The PhoB

☞

The Philosophy

of

BEING

How to Be Your
Authentic BEING

Free Your BEING
From Your Mind's

Matrix

A Manual for Liberating Your BEING From Your Matrix:

Do You Believe What Language Leads You to Believe?

Are You a True-Believer

of

The Products of Language and Thought?

Presented by

the BEING @ Professor BEING

Dedication

**This manual is dedicated to
the LIVING-BEINGS of EARTH.
May we evolve to live in harmony
with each other and with THAT
which sustains us all.**

<><><>

Table of Contents

The I-AM We Are

I have gone where words would have me go.
To the moods and modes they'd have of me.
Yet, at last, HERE I am, free to simply be
WHAT I am beyond those moods and modes
Dictated by the believed 'things' of mind.

HERE, I am the I-AM,
As you find your I-AM to be.
I do not so much think of WHAT I am,
As do I meditate upon these mind-made
movements,
For which I am no longer pushed and pulled,
Goaded, swayed, forced, and told,
Formed, shaped, sourced, and molded,
Trimmed, shaved, monied, and enslaved
By the 'worlds' of words.

For, I have slipped away into this HERE...
Slipped from these confinements to this PLACE,
This eternal HAVEN, this ever-present SPACE
Where I need not keep up the exhausting pace
Of this orchestrated run, this winless race,
Organized for those who play 'human race'.

There are no here-afters,
Somewhere above the rafters.
We need not wait to touch, see, and hear
This miraculous and havenly HERE.

We were of IT before we came.
We are of IT as we remain.
We will be of IT as we sustain
The living GARDEN, the wondrous refrain,
That needs no words to be.

Come, come along with me
So that we may simply be
The I-AM we most naturally are,
All of us, from near and far.

The purpose of this manual is to lead us to a necessary relationship with the mind, one we must have if we are to achieve our fullest actualization as BEINGS in LIFE.

Preface

<In order to present this manual, I have to play with words.>

The reason for starting this manual off with this previous sentence should become clear by the time its last sentence is achieved.

This much I will say right now:

THAT to which these words would lead you is not itself a factor of words!

In order to help anyone (especially, at a distance) to an actualization of our true BEINGNESS, one is compelled to use the medium of language. As we journey through the byways of the following words, one can only hope that the reader will eventually actualize WHAT these words are intended to indicate, then, to have less need for them and, ideally, to leave them behind. This would be done by, figuratively speaking, stepping out of a personal 'world' of words and beworded thoughts into the simplicity, clarity, and ineffableness of being all-HERE, which I have come to call simply, after a fair number of personal epiphanies, "being a BEING".

And, it is indeed "simple" to achieve such spiritual-mental liberation or mastery. There are no esoteric rules or laws, no mysterious secrets, or cryptic, hidden knowledge for recognizing one's BEINGNESS. One need only establish a proper relationship with the mind, with one's biocomputer, that piece of biological equipment that transforms sensory data into mental maps. This proper relationship prevents one's BEING from getting bogged down in the notion that there is "reality" in the mind. Erroneously called "enlightenment", "higher consciousness", "nirvana", such spiritual liberation is simply being liberated from the notion (knowtion) that the mind can or does contain "reality". This is no "higher consciousness". This is simply the achievement of <u>consciousness</u>, of which, for being so lost in the believed 'worlds' of beworded thought, the typical citizen is bereft and in need.

It does not so much matter what we call IT. What matters more than anything else in LIFE is whether or not we are indeed HERE as BEINGS. For, without such actualization, ALL, eventually, is lost... not only for the individual, but with our impact as a species, for the ecologies of a once thriving WORLD.

Everything from living as a wholly fulfilled BEING to being fully alive in this MIRACLE of our

BIOSPHERE depends upon our being aware of our essential BEINGNESS. Without such awareness, we can—in our ignorance—only come to destroy THAT upon which we are most essentially dependent.

"But of what are we ignorant?" one may ask.

First of all, we may be ignorant of the EXISTENCE of our most essential and basic BEINGNESS, as individuals or as entities who are contiguous with this greater COMMUNITY that we may call "LIFE on Earth". To be modern in our nomenclature, we may call this COMMUNITY our "BIOSPHERE". Whatever we do call IT, one thing remains certain, IT is HERE all around us, as a LIVING-WORLD that has, at the furthest reaches of thought or cognition, an infinite improbability of existing. For this reason alone, it behooves me to call this COMMUNITY a "MIRACLE"... a MIRACLE which extends throughout the farthest depths and heights of this BIOSPHERE.

I have played with words for some years now. This last utterance is as succinct as I can be with respect to the foundation for all the other words that are contained herein.

On The Communication of Ideas

With respect to the communication of ideas, especially those that could lead a reader or listener to "consciousness", I am ever aware of how attached people are to their current verbiage, the verbal structures, of their own minds. I have had many a long mutually sincere discussion with people who can only receive what I have to present as foreign, disruptive, or even threatening to a well-worked, well-established matrix of mental structures, which (coincidentally) provides the means for imagined security for physical and/or spiritual survival.

The structure of an individual's systems of thinking may be likened to a house of cards. Intellectual and spiritual exploration requires one to analyze and reorganize one's *house*. Thus, intellectual-spiritual discourse requires a special kind of mental discipline. Challenging and achieving growth therein, refreshing the matrix of one's established thoughts, is not easy for many an individual... especially, those who depend upon believed stories, doctrine, and dogma for their current psychological well-being.

When one approaches one's personal *house* and wishes to communicate, one comes to the fortunate discovery that our communications are often limited to sharing noises that we call "words". [I like to call them "noisetools".] Yet, if we wish to adequately communicate with these noises, we need to come to terms with what they can and cannot do. The first problem surfaces when we appreciate that the noises we emit do not in themselves convey meaning. Rather, they trigger reactions in our separate minds. These reactions are the <u>private meanings</u> that we conjure as a result of the unique experiences that each of us brings to the present moment. **In short, ultimately, meanings are not in words, they are in minds— minds that are all significantly unique with regard to interpretation and reaction.**

With meaning being ultimately in the individual mind, what can we hope to accomplish by sharing our noises or their reflections in print? What benefit is there to listening to the noises of someone like me who would stand before an audience? I will assert that we can hope at least to be stimulated, so to think within our own singular systems of thinking, so to come to better manage and master our own processes of thinking.

In that systems of personal meaning, in themselves, cannot be conveyed by the mere utterance of noisetools, it should be understood that a 'state' of mind—and, even more ineffably so, a PROCESS of BEING—should not be expected to be transferred or conveyed, merely by listening to someone uttering noisetools... or, of course, by reading such noises codified in print.

However, to this author's pleasure certain bits of "wisdom", certain well-placed formulas of thought, can lead the individual to her/his own psychological or spiritual liberation... synonymously, to her/his own BEING-fulfillment, BEING-actualization.

I am suggesting here that some verbal phrases or concepts can act as "seed-formulas" in the mind, thereby, to have a powerful effect upon the thinking system, the psyche, and life of the individual cultivating such a formula. As the reader will come to appreciate, for our purposes, the most powerful of seed-formulas for achieving BEING-actualization are those which use "negations". A negation is simply a statement that says that something is not the case, is not true.

All things are dear, not for their own sake, but for the sake of the Being. This Being alone exists everywhere. It <u>cannot</u> be understood or known, for It alone is the Understander and the Knower. Its nature <u>cannot</u> be said to be positively as such. It is realized through endless denials as "<u>not this</u>, <u>not that</u>". The Being is self-luminous, indestructible, unthinkable.

—Yajnavalkya of Vedic India, circa 3100 years ago.

In other words, if one is seeking the broad equanimity and contentment of fully being one's own BEING, one can do so by using certain negations. Via the mechanisms of direct or indirect negations, this manual will guide a reader to the spiritual liberation that is being called "being a BEING", herein. Should you, dear reader, be so interested, you will shortly have a mastery of such negations.

The Perennial Concern

I just introduced a one Yajnavalkya of Vedic India. There are untold numbers of BEINGS who have tried to help humanity achieve the clarity of being all-HERE. Many people have dedicated their lives to popularizing methods which aid our BEING in thinking in ways which make it easier to appreciate that our BEING is not ITSELF some 'thing' that the mind can hold. The list is very long. Many have appreciated how important it is to teach us so-called *humans* how to be of pure and unadulterated BEINGNESS. In order that we may live in peace and harmony—today, even, in ecological harmony, we must come to see through the entirety of the mind's 'things' to the wondrous and extensive BEING that constitutes our true EXISTENCE. As creatures who tend to worship the creations of our own minds, we must come to see beyond all the covertly divisive 'things' of mind to an appreciation of this openly natural, living, and holistic WORLD within which we all live interdependently. As emphasized, as a result of the impact that humans are having upon these ecological systems, the biological welfare of our WORLD is, itself, being threatened by the rigid mannerisms of those who have not as yet had the opportunity to actualize themselves as BEINGS in a WORLD of BEING.

In the East, our ways have been edified by teachers like Lao Tzu or Laozi (who may have been a mythological and/or composite figure of the Zhou Dynasty of China, 1046-256 BCE) and Sakyamuni (aka Gautama Buddha, 563-483 BCE) . In the West, outstanding figures like Francis Bacon (1561-1626) right on through phenomenological philosophers like Immanuel Kant (1724-1804) and Jean-Paul Sartre (1905-1980), onto popularizers like Alfred Korzybski of General Semantics (1879-1950) and the excellent interpreter of Eastern wisdom, Alan Watts (1915-1973), come to mind.

If the reader were to start an associative journey with any of these, s/he would discover the workings of other thinkers who have shown interest in thinking in ways that would liberate us from rigid patterns of thinking, thus to achieve, per this manual, being BEINGS who are all-HERE.

Of course, in order to obtain a prominent place in one's thinking, the seeds of wisdom need nurturing such that they can actually have a positive effect on the mental managements of the average citizen. If they find "fertile" mental ground, the seeds can be prolific agents for change. If we are unable to cultivate them because of some blockage stemming from our current 'states' of mind, the seeds of wisdom will not obtain their due prominence in our lives. However, the mind is an amazing thing. Given a good suggestion, it seems to adapt fairly well; if not immediately. Often enough, with a little coaxing and a little thoughtful consideration, it eventually takes hold. We do reap what we sow in the mind. I suspect that anyone who would be interested in having this book would be ready to reap WHAT its words sow.

It is my hope that the words herein will adequately lead you, dear reader, to a PLACE from which the intended "meaning" of these 'word-things' will be discerned. I can only hope that the means for bringing you to this PLACE are adequate to their purpose.

On the Distribution of this Book

We live in a world in which the ownership and control of money seems too frequently to take precedence over all other concerns. What concerns the author of this book is not money. Now that I am in the autumn of this life, I am even more concerned with matters of greater import than the transitory values of money.

In that we come into this world naked and leave with nothing, leaving, as it happens, even without our nakedness, I am concerned with what we are to leave behind. I am of the opinion that what remains of us has more to do with what we have given for the furtherance of LIFE than what we have been able to hoard for the time-being. There was a time when some very wise peoples saw ownership by the few as a disease. To maintain sustenance, these looked to the then more diversely abundant creations of LIFE, to find a cornucopia of interactive provisions. These peoples even prayed to the "spirits" that resided in the natural world about them. And, for such reverence, they were able to strike a balance within their environs that allowed for an appreciation for the holistic LIVING-

SYSTEMS that provided them sustenance. Yet, as humans got ever more proficient within their exploitations, such wisdom continuously waned. Step-by-step (speaking, figuratively and literally), such wisdom would remain only in certain regions about the world, only in outlying areas, only with those who were able to remain isolated from those eyes that saw everything, even members of their own kind, merely as "resources".

Today, in spite of the fact that there are alternative technologies for peoples to work in community towards preserving and sustaining the biologies of a planet, there is not enough wisdom for the will to broadly and earnestly implement such technologies. Out of ignorance and habit, we human beings are unable to raise this planet's LIVING-SYSTEMS to a level where THEY are not subordinate to the exploitations and resource-needs of our non-living systems. The technologies of such systems go onward without the implementation of ecologically sound overviews and managements. As an example, the FORESTS of our planet continue to be seen as just so much 'wood' to be consumed by these systems. In the past, the construction of fleet upon sunken fleet of wooden ships gobbled up FORESTS. Today, under the forces of rampantly growing, global, laissez-faire consumption, there are those who cannot wait to get the teeth of their saws and automated jaws into the remaining virgin FORESTS of our WORLD. The list of other examples is long, yet, easily enough listed by anyone who is awakening to the biological disruptions on this planet.

Yet, in these newly ever rebooting 'worlds' of ours, we are blessed with new and ever expanding sources of information, all of which is available at the tips of our tapping and clicking fingers. And, such availability is for the most part free. Although a financial challenge for the authors, artists, and providers of such information, the Internet has the potential of greatly helping to awaken the teeming masses of *human beings* to the fact that our interactive BEING requires attention and reverence for a sustainable future.

Thank you for your interest in The PhoB and for helping to distribute the news that we can all be HERE, together, as BEINGS, in an ecologically sustainable WORLD.

What we do for the least of us, we do for all of us.

...

[Please, see the Appendix for how single quotation marks and all-caps are being used in this manual.]

<>
<>
<>

"It's the world that has been pulled over your eyes to blind you from the truth."

"What truth?"

"... that you are a slave, Neo. Like everyone else, you were born into bondage, born into a prison that you cannot smell, or taste, or touch... a prison for your mind."

—quoted from the movie The Matrix

...

You knock at the door of pure-EXISTENCE,
shake your thought-wings, loosen your shoulders, and open.

—Jelaluddin Rumi, 13th century Sufi poet,
from the poem "Say I Am You"
[as translated by Coleman Barks]*

* The author took the liberty to change the translation, so to include the phrase "pure-EXISTENCE", so to better express the message of this manual.

...

For one rings like a cracked bell when s/he thinks and acts with a split mind—one part standing aside to interfere with the other, to control, to condemn, or to admire.

—Alan W. Watts

Come to manage the 'things' of your mind;
don't let them manage you. It's that simple.

—Professor BEING

Good News! Finally!

Here's the manual on how to manage the mind

that you didn't get at birth.

Introduction

The opening into complete FULLNESS,
into this expansive EVERYTHINGNESS,
into this wondrous BEINGNESS, may be labeled
'inner emptiness', 'no-mindness', 'nothingness'–
these labels themselves being merely other mind-
made 'things'. It may involve not believing any
'thing' of the artificial, virtual 'worlds' of mind.
The opening to beyond the mind's facade does not
matter; 'what' we pass through does not matter.
What matters is that we come to be BEINGS who
are entirely HERE beyond the facade.

Everyone has her/his own opening!

The Opposite of Being Fully Your BEING, of Being All HERE, is to Live <u>Unconsciously</u> in a 'World' of Virtual-Being

We cannot change the fact that we function in 'worlds' of virtual-being. That is not doable. However, while functioning within these 'worlds' of virtual-being, we can, nonetheless, be aware of that fact and, most importantly, of the additional fact that <u>our true BEING-in-ITSELF is not virtual</u>. And, even more importantly, we can become aware of how we do ourselves, our own BEING, great disservice when we treat ourselves and each other as though we were merely virtual 'things' in digital games of civil being.

▶ **We are non-virtual BEINGS functioning virtually in a non-virtual WORLD.**

We are <u>non-virtual</u> BEINGS that remain hidden in-full-view within or behind the perceived <u>virtual</u> 'things' of our minds. As BEINGS of the true, non-virtual FABRIC of pure-EXISTENCE, we must relate and interrelate via the mechanisms of the perceptions and conceptions of the mind-body. The developments of our perceptions cannot be other than virtual—as are all the 'products' that might represent some THING or BEING. The picture in my hand and the picture in the back of my mind have something very important in common: as representations they are both virtual 'things', while the THINGS or BEINGS beyond them are never virtual.

We live as non-virtual BEINGS who–if we are to express ourselves, so to be recognized as being HERE, so to be heard–must act upon the ever-present stages of these theaters of virtual-being. Yet, as I hold someone's hand and, thereby, recognize her or his presence as being HERE, I am given direct evidence that beyond these virtual perceptions, beyond the mentally contrived show of my virtual-being, beyond the thought-up projections of this biocomputer, there exists a wondrous, unadulterated EXISTENCE within which we are all wondrous BEINGS. I cannot, I wish not, and I will not ever confuse these mind-made perceptions with the actual, true, pure, and unsullied BEING that is holding my hand!

While our perceptions are never equivalent to any THING or BEING, we can, nevertheless, use our perceptions to recognize that our non-virtual, true, noumenal BEING is HERE. Even as I recognize that the images in the mirrors of my life are not WHO I am, nevertheless, I still recognize that it is my BEING who is doing the recognizing. We are HERE before and beyond all these 'things' of mind! We are HERE, in spite of all these 'things'!

Once we fully appreciate that we exist beyond these mental 'things', especially, beyond the beworded 'things', we shortly come to appreciate that all THINGS and all BEINGS exist, in-their-own-right, beyond the limited enclosures of mind. We rest in this SPOT and we have the epiphany that all which is

HERE is also, always, beyond the presumptuous projections of mind. For all its utilities, the mind can only do us disservice when we are unable to behold this ineffable PLACE which ultimately contains our own ineffable BEING.

This manual is putting forth the proposition that we cannot be fulfilled in LIFE if we are unable to fully behold our ineffable and unadulterated BEING. This manual presents a collection of words the purpose of which is to lead us to an actualization of being fully HERE as BEINGS who thrive by living beyond the beworded 'things' so dutifully employed by the mind.

If we follow consciousness back to its origins, we find that it emanates from some THING that has been ever beyond the ken of consciousness. For, from ITSELF, from this THING, emanates consciousness. Herein, that some THING is being called "BEING". It's been called other names. It's been called Spirit, the Soul, the I-am, Psyche, Atman, etc.. As used herein, the term "BEING" owes ITS <u>verbal</u> origin to the simple ACTUALITY of the universal BEING that is in and of us all. [Please, lift your head up from reading. Behold, it is your BEING that does that.]

I use the term "BEING", herein, not to indulge in metaphysics. This term and any of its synonyms could lead to metaphysical and philosophical discussion or debate. So be it. Yet, there is no need for such debate, for the word "BEING" is meant to refer simply to that nondescript or indescribable WHATEVER that is recognized as the "I-that-I-most-purely-am". No one can describe this ULTIMATE-I, whence IT came, or just how extensive IT is. Being beyond conceptualization, our BEING cannot be pinned down by words or thought. Playing with theologies, cosmologies, or philosophies can only produce human-made, artificial attributions, yet, HERE IT is and HERE WE are, anyway, in spite of all the verbiage that we merely lug about.

What IT is and how IT came into being is inscrutable. And for the purposes of this manual, which tries not to delve into belief systems, such contemplation is irrelevant or immaterial, and unimportant. I suggest simply that our BEING is equally in and of every LIVING-THING, and, at least, potentially, in and of THAT which is called "non-living"... whatever THAT may be. For me personally, I consider our BEING to be of that indefinable ULTIMATE GROUND or URGE of EXISTENCE that, often enough, demonstrates the uncanny capacity for being aware of what IT thinks and does—and, with a little insight, can achieve BEING-actualization.

BEING?

Let's look closely at this noisetool "BEING" (all in capital letters):

With this term, I wish to point at your BEING, as well as at mine—at our BEING, so to suggest that we are of the LIFE that lies beyond the limitations introduced as we *think* of and about our BEING. I wish to point at that ultimate WHATEVER that resides HERE, as LIVING-BEINGS, beyond all symbol and contemplation.

▶If only all of us could see IT and, better, consciously be IT!

Ideas, concepts, or mental 'things' suggested by noises like 'I', 'me', 'we', or 'they' can never do our BEING justice. What's more, any thoughts <u>that are believed</u> to relate to our true BEING, to mine, yours, or anyone's BEING, can do no more than limit us to the confines of mind-conceived illusions, often enough illusions that are stubbornly held by people locked in and suffering from being in mental 'worlds'.

I have made it a mission of my life to understand the mechanisms or <u>semantic ingredients</u> for achieving BEING-fulfillment, BEING-actualization. In this presentation, I attempt to clarify the basic ingredients of how to manage one's mind and, thus, one's language-influenced thoughts, so to establish a clear understanding of how to be fully our BEING.

The Value of These Words

As implied in this manual, one cannot share a PROCESS of BEING by simply sharing words. Regardless of the unfortunate fact that words **cannot show anyone explicitly how to be of BEING, how to be all-HERE,** the value of this manual comes from how it can guide the reader to pass through her/his own thought-up 'selves' into this unthought WORLD of BEING. While being prompted to see language and beworded thought for what they are and are not capable, the reader comes to put them in their proper place (occasionally, even aside)... thereby, freeing the BEING to be all-HERE. This manual provides certain suggestions that the reader can use to navigate beyond her/his own thinking-system, when reified (believed), beyond her/his own mind-engendered matrix.

> [To reify a 'thing' of mind (like a word, a thought, or a concept, for instance) is to take it to be identical or equivalent to a BEING or THING of the actual WORLD. A simple example of a reification is recognized when one *thinks* a thought to be about the "reality" of someone. The verbal formulas, "He is a white man", "She is a nice piece of ass", "He is a black man", "He is an enemy", "She is a Tutsi", "He is a Jew", "That is a tree", "He is a terrorist" are all demonstrating how concepts are *thought* into being, are reified into being, confused with living BEINGS!

Yes, those BEINGS called "trees" are living BEINGS, deserving to be beheld as such!

The predominant reason that this manual exists is to help eliminate the insufferable tendency to which we humans are exposed when we are caused to confuse the 'things' of our minds with the BEINGS of our WORLD. In the opinion of the author, reification is the most wide-spread and egregious of all the recognized errors (dys-eases) of reasoning.

As the reader will see, the author is publishing a thesis with this manual, The Reification-Extinction Thesis, which purports that the most fundamental reason for the major mass extinction, taking place on Earth right now, is due to our inability (as a species) to see beyond the reifications of our everyday functions to the biological-ecological systems of our planet. See the Appendix for a presentation on the issues of reification and dereification (the latter being the cure for the dys-ease of reification.)]

In other words, this manual can help the reader to dereify (de-reify, un-believe) the 'things' of her/his thinking system, so eventually to graduate from her or his own relatively fixed school of thought. By using the noisetools, herein, s/he—with a little attention, effort, and practice—will come to be a BEING who is fulfilled in being all-HERE.

After having examined all those 'things'—all those images, thoughts, and words—that hang like ornaments from our trees of knowledge, after having explored the limited contours of language and thought, after having placed all those 'things' in their proper place or, perhaps, in oblivion—where many of them belong—or, perhaps, merely in storage for some future construction of new symbolisms, neologisms, syllogisms, thoughts, mental 'maps', myths, and rituals for the games and plays of our theaters (of the Shakespearean stage or of the street), at some point, the reader will find her/his BEING standing HERE, standing unadulterated, spiritually free, and complete, where all frontiers have dissolved away into an expansive MULTIVERSE of a most extensive and actualized BEING.

As most of us wish to live authentically, let's see how our curiosity is piqued by the idea of being a BEING. This manual offers the means for the reader to escape the matrix of the mind—if s/he hasn't already done so.

—the BEING @Professor BEING, 2000

I am dust particles in sunlight.
I am the round sun.
To the bits of dust I say, "Stay."
To the sun, "Keep moving."*

I am morning mist, and the breathing of
evening.
I am wind in the top of a grove, and surf on the
cliff.
Mast, rudder, helmsman, and keel.
I am also the coral reef on which they founder.

I am a tree with a trained parrot in its
branches.
Silence, thought, and voice.
The musical air coming through a flute,
a spark of a stone, a flickering in metal.
Both candle, and the moth crazy around it.
Rose, and nightingale lost in the fragrance.
I am all orders of being, the circling galaxy,
the evolutionary intelligence, the lift, and the
falling away.
What is, and what isn't.
You who know Jelaluddin, you the one in all,
say who I am.

Say I am You.

—Jelaluddin Rumi

(as translated by Coleman Barks)

*Obviously, the sun is only "moving" relative to one who sees it moving across
the sky. Hundreds of years after Jelaluddin made this wonderfully poetic
utterance of his monistic spirituality, we humans were finally permitted to
accept the fact that it was us who were moving through a never-ending arc,
while the sun remained relatively stationary.

I celebrate myself, and sing myself,
And what I assume you shall assume,
For every atom belonging to me as good belongs to you.

—Walt Whitman

(from the poem "Song of Myself")

The PhoB

The Philosophy of BEING

Being Your Authentic BEING

A Presentation

About Being Fully Your BEING

As mentioned, the term "BEING" is written in capital letters to remind the reader's BEING that our BEING should always be viewed as an inconceivable, non-conceptualizable, indivisible WHOLE that is ever greater than the sum of ITS mentally conceived 'parts'. When I use the capitalized letters "B-E-I-N-G", I am <u>not</u> referring to what one *thinks* one is. On the contrary, I am referring to THAT which one ultimately is—without the accouterments or projections of mind. I am referring to that WHATEVER that we are— before we try to label or describe the BEING with our words and thoughts. I am referring to the true BEING, not to the conceptual version, not to a 'figment' of virtual-being, not to some 'self' conjured in thought and mind, not to those ephemeral 'reflections' into which we *think* our BEING.

I am referring to WHAT we are in between, before, after, and beyond our thoughts!

I am referring to WHAT we are in spite of our thoughts, with or without the urgency that our thinking may give them.

Those who use the mind as though its screenings can reflect BEING, are, albeit unintentionally, doing IT a great disservice; for the mind's "screenings" can only act like bubbles of 'virtual-being' around our BEING, never can they truly stand for IT. In order to become fully conscious of being all-HERE, these bubbles of defined and believed screenings must be seen for 'what' they are. One can take them off to look at them for what they are: mind-generated creations, fictions, illusions that can too easily build a matrix in the omni-theater of a mind. When one becomes adept at doing this ultimately simple and eventually pleasurable operation, one will be able to step into this ever-present BEINGNESS, into the original, authentic, unadulterated HERE, beyond all the busy, beworded 'things' of mind.

►Matrix: a new word for helping us manage the mind

The concept of the matrix (as suggested in the movie of that title) stands as an appropriate allegory for something that is actually happening in our lives, something that remains, unfortunately and too commonly, beyond the ken of too many humans.

As used in the movie, the term "matrix" has wonderful potential for giving a new twist to an old idea. With the potential of a new interpretation, "matrix" can become a new verbal tool (a neologism), one that is well-needed within common speech.[1] It can become a newly accepted word for a fresh understanding of our truest EXISTENCE, which will be soon ours.

►Some 'things' just need a little fine tuning.

For those who have not seen the movie or who need a refresher, in The Matrix, computerized machines evolve to have a superior form of artificial intelligence, which produces its own collective *consciousness* with its own drive for survival. The intelligent machines come to view the humans as just another example of that inferior stuff called "life". Of course, with such an

---

1   Coincidentally, the hero of the story of The Matrix is named "Neo". "Matrix" is Neo's neologism.

attitude, war ensues between the humans and the machines.

The machines win. However, during the course of the war, the humans try to kill the machines off by blotting out the sun, the source of energy for the machines. Needing energy to survive, the intelligent machines have to figure out how to get a constant fix of electrical power. Eureka! The human body transforms food into electrical energy; thus, the machines realize they can grow humans to provide a good source of power. Therefore, instead of removing the vermin from the planet, once and for always, the intelligent machines devise a way to use their output of electrical energy. They will harness that output. The humans are to be used as "batteries" to help keep the machines alive in a darkness that the humans created. From the viewpoint of the machines, this is good recycling! Oh, the justice of it! Oh, the irony of it!

In order to sap their output, the machines must hook the humans up to the grid. To do this, they must keep them in one fixed place. And, in order to do that, the machines must keep the humans quiet and still, in suspended animation, in pods that will keep their bodies alive. However, there is a small problem. The machines soon appreciate that, even though they can override the senses and perceptions of the humans, easily enough, they still must provide their minds with some kind of stimulus. While creating and experimenting with artificial, mental *experience*, the machines soon appreciate that not just any *experience* will do. They must provide the humans with <u>virtual lives</u> that act to challenge their minds, adequately enough, so that the humans do not die, shall we say, "from boredom".

The genius of the movie, The Matrix, reveals itself not only in its extraordinary cinematographic animation and special effects, but, also, in how the artists were able to create such a marvelous allegory that so well parallels a governing but often hidden influence within the human condition. As mentioned, the existence of the movie's "matrix" <u>indirectly</u> suggests that we regular human beings are, in fact, living lives of "virtual-being" without, of course, being aware of it.

Virtual!?! Yes, virtual.

Although we exist in a WORLD of actual substance, of matter and energies, our experience of all THIS is always reduced—by way of the sensory and cognitive functions of the mind—to these virtual 'things' in a virtual theater of mind.

As it turns out, the machines are up to the task. They are not only able to hardwire connections to the human nervous system and to feed it complex programming, they are able to create a matrix of marvelous facsimile, incorporating believable virtual 'worlds' that succeed in fooling the humans into feeling sufficiently alive. Thus, the matrix guarantees the steady flows of the vital juices (so to speak) of the "batteries" and, consequently, the continued flows of the electrical juice needed from the farms where the humans are being born, grown, and tapped.

In summary, having won the war against the humans, the intelligent machines come to harness the bodies of humans as a source of electrical energy. In order to allow the humans to stay in one spot—a spot from which the machines can sap the voltaic energy they need, the triumphant machines cleverly devise sophisticated programming that can mimic an entire virtual 'world' within which millions of human-batteries can subsist as slaves. This virtual 'world' is to be called "the matrix". However, in accord with "human nature", this 'world' cannot be too perfect; for, a 'world' without problems offers no challenges and humans just do not fare all that well without having challenges.

No problem! The machines make a "matrix" that is more perfect by virtue of the existence of imperfections that cause challenges, challenges that create ups and downs in their virtual lives, challenges that generate fears for which they may be saved, perhaps even, by their own invention. The machines are successful. They fool the humans into believing the matrix and into remaining good batteries. The machines get the electrical energy needed for the grid.

In the movie, a grand 'world' of virtual-being is imposed upon the humans by way of direct connections being hardwired to the human nervous system. Interestingly enough, for us who are also taken over by artificial 'worlds', there is something similar going on. It's just that the mechanism for taking over the mind and nervous system is different. The mechanism does not involve hardwiring and externally imposed programming. Rather, each person unconsciously develops her/his own matrix in her/his own mind by implementing a flawed and deceptive mental process called "reification", which is a special form of belief whereby one confuses pure-EXISTENCE with one's own mind-made 'things'.

On the planet Earth, the individual is exposed to all kinds of subtle and not-so subtle persuasions, derived from different cultures, languages, institutions, schools of thought, customs, habits, et cetera. From such exposure, each of us builds and adopts a virtual-world. As such a fabricated 'world' is composed of a large representational structure made of impressions, of still or moving images and of words, it must be virtual. Yet, the mind (and nervous system) of someone is not "taken over" just because it produces virtual 'things'. Rather, one's mind is taken over when the 'things' of one's 'world' are not recognized as functionally being only "virtual"—this because of how the 'things' are fixedly "believed" (reified).

►Our minds are taken over because we believe the 'products' of mind to be "real".

When the 'things' of a mental 'world' are believed, when they are *thought* to relate to "reality", they are no longer questioned. When the 'things' of one's thoughts are *thought* "real"—when they are believed, one does not challenge them for their symbolic, hypothetical, or provisional value. Thus, in order to make a matrix for a regular human being, the 'things' of a virtual mental 'world' and that 'world', itself, must be believed or reified into being considered equivalent to the actual WORLD. With just a little insight, we can see just how potentially dangerous such reifying processes can be to the welfare of any BEING or community of BEINGS. The DOLPHINS of our WORLD are still being slaughtered in spite of how millions of other BEINGS are begging they be not seen (reified into being seen) as merely 'food'.

Thus, we see how easily we so-called "humans" are caused to confuse a WHAT of pure-EXISTENCE with the 'whats' of the mind!

►*Humans* project the 'whats' of mind onto WHAT is outside of mind!

Obviously, such confusion works upon one's mind in unseen ways. For instance, one is typically unaware of how *believing is seeing*—<u>per the classifications and definitions</u> that the mind projects upon the THINGS and BEINGS of the WORLD. How easily we are programmed into seeing a fellow BEING as just a 'unit of labor', as a killable 'enemy', as merely a consumable 'food', or as just so much 'lumber' that so readily causes FORESTS to be converted into 'money'!

The power of reification to blind us to the presence of THIS, our extensive BEINGNESS, to cause us to view our mental 'things' as equal to the THINGS of pure-EXISTENCE, is most compelling, often overwhelming, and nearly always devastating. Easily taken for granted and even *thought* necessary or required for living—by those who inadvertently push for believing mind-made 'things', this mechanism of belief, known as "reification", causes us to frequently forget that the WORLD (the UNIVERSE or EXISTENCE) is indeed never able to be squeezed into the mind!

► **The mind contains its own 'things';
it does not contain pure-EXISTENCE.**

The trick to living successfully—as individuals and as a species—is to use the 'things' of the mind to sustain the LIVING-SYSTEMS of this WORLD. It is not to use the mind to reify its own 'things' thus to supplant the BEINGS of a planet with its own nonliving, mind-held 'things'. To do so, at first, may seem practical; but, in the long-run, just how practical is it to replace the LIVING-SYSTEMS of a planet with non-living operations that waste and destroy those SYSTEMS?

[As a preliminary to what is presented further along in this manual, we may remind ourselves as to how the scientific method is still being poorly applied in our everyday psychological, sociological and ecological lives. For some centuries, now, those who use the scientific method have hoped that humans may eventually come to better manage the mind's symbolic-representational-provisional-virtual-hypothetical structures.]

Most troublesome is how we humans use language. As we use words, we tend to *believe* the verbal structures we invent to be about "reality". We believe that the words—the names, labels, definitions, descriptions and stories used to build our personal 'worlds'—have something to do with that notion of "reality". We project these 'worlds' unto the WORLD about us, such that we become unable to behold the pure-EXISTENCE of the LIVING-SYSTEMS of our WORLD. We become so inured to believing the 'worlds' of our word-filled minds, we become unable to see beyond the filters of our own words—of our linguistic inventions and self-imposed languages. In this manner, we become subjugated to our own verbal inventions, to the believed (reified) structures built from all the words housed in our minds. As we believe (reify) the mind's verbally defined imagery, as we take the verbally generated 'worlds' to be about "reality", we become convinced that our mental 'worlds' are the one-and-only genuine "reality" to be had. Thus, via such belief (such reification), each of us makes a personal matrix which acts as a "prison for the mind" and, thus, also, ever so egregiously, for our spiritually unliberated BEING. Unfortunately, the average, true-believing citizen is unaware of the prison (for the mind), the personal matrix into which s/he has thought (believed) her/his own BEING.

▶ **When a virtual-world is believed, one becomes a prisoner of a personal matrix!**

Of course, the movie gives hope for freeing the enslaved multitudes, for releasing the batteries from their pods of servitude, for returning to them their now latent, as-yet unactualized, prominence consistent with our original drive for authentic experience, or, for, shall we say, "Freedom". Within that theme, along comes our newly freed, bewildered yet heroic protagonist, Neo (the new guy from the blocks of pods.). This maverick ex-battery is going to prove to be too clever for the computers' own good. He is going to see the programming for 'what' it is—just so much projected illusion and virtual display. Most importantly, he is going to be able to show that the matrix can be stopped in its tracks.

...

How are we to stop the self-deluding programming of our 'worlds'?

The answer. With a little guidance, each of us can free our own BEING from having to accept that our true BEING is ITSELF equivalent to the virtual-being that our minds and nervous systems generate. Such guidance points out a relatively simple fact that is expressed in different ways, with different words.

We can:

1. ...stop <u>fixedly</u> imposing words onto our experience, so to behold the undefined WORLD within which we truly live.

2. ...step out of the believed (reified) 'things' of mind into the dereified HERE.

3. ...see the projections of mind for 'what' they are, to actualize the MIRACLE of pure-EXISTENCE all about.

4. ...achieve BEING-actualization.

▶**When we stop projecting our believed 'things' onto pure-EXISTENCE, we pass from <u>believing the virtual-beingness</u> of our minds <u>to being BEINGS</u> in the full and actual glory of LIFE.**

A Relatively Simple Precept/Principle

As the reader will see, the endeavor of freeing one's BEING from a personal matrix, of being fully one's BEING, can be much easier if one can come to appreciate and use one relatively simple precept (or principle), <u>one simple seed-formula</u>:

"The 'thought' is <u>not</u> the THING."

This seed-formula is, in effect, all one would need in order to start to become BEING-actualized, to embark upon being all-HERE. Often enough we are given, from left, right, and in-between, quite a variety of principles to live by. And, these principles surely have their importance; however, living is complicated enough. Wouldn't it be nice to have just one simple precept to live by... one that would, practically, do the job for the rest of those that purport to lead us to a better PLACE? The above seed-formula does the job, but a simple idea is not necessarily easy until one "gets it" and, then, cultivates its application. Mind you, simplicity does not necessarily become easy without practice.

This manual was crafted to help the reader self-prepare her/his own mind to "see" and, eventually, to be all-HERE. The above seed-formula is intended to do just that.

By the way, there are variations of this primary seed-formula that help with achieving a proper outlook. Observe how the benefits of negation can help us:

"The 'symbolic structure' is <u>not</u> the THING symbolized."

-or-

"Our 'thoughts' do <u>not</u> constitute pure-EXISTENCE."

-or-

"The 'map' is <u>not</u> the TERRITORY."

[This last seed-formula was provided by Alfred Korzybski, the founder of General Semantics.]

Nicely enough, this latter variation is somewhat concrete and easy to visualize. It should be interpreted as:

"Our mental 'maps' (the thoughts, the 'what's' of mind) are not equivalent to WHAT exists in pure-EXISTENCE."

That "WHAT"— being synonymous with the actual THINGS or TERRITORY of pure EXISTENCE—lies independently out HERE, beyond all the potentially reified 'things' of mind.

Some times it helps to make advice more personal. For that reason, the reader may prefer an iteration of the above principle that relates more operatively to one's own person. Thus, we have the following:

"I am not what I think I am."

Of course, we can fit other pronouns into this personally proactive principle and it still stands:

"YOU are not what YOU think YOU are."

-or-

"WE are not what WE think WE are."

Moreover, by extension:

"WE are not what anyone thinks WE are."

How can the above seed-formulas lead one to being all-HERE?

Again, by using the saving grace of negation [The 'thought' is <u>not</u> the THING. I am <u>not</u> what I think I am.], we are eventually led to a conclusion, to an actual PLACE, wherein no affirmations of thought and mind are accepted as able to replace WHAT is HERE all around us—HERE where the pure-EXISTENCE of our BEING thrives—in spite of all the mind-made 'things' that would cause us to *think* our BEING into being merely equivalent to some artificial, virtual 'things' made-in-mind.

Let's revisit the negations of Yajnavalkya:

> **All things are dear, not for their own sake, but for the sake of the Being. This Being alone exists everywhere. It <u>cannot</u> be understood or known, for It alone is the Understander and the Knower. Its nature <u>cannot</u> be said to be positively as such. It is realized through endless denials as "<u>not this, not that</u>". The Being is self-luminous, indestructible, unthinkable.**

—Yajnavalkya

In order to be all-HERE (to be actualized in BEING), one must use the mind (brain, biocomputer) appropriately. The appropriate manner of using the mind is to use it as an apparatus, as a piece of biological equipment, that makes <u>symbolic or representational structures</u> of the data coming from our senses and memories. [Again, the term "mental 'map'" may be a more visually concrete synonym for "symbolic or representational structure".] It is of utmost importance to our overall well-being to appreciate that our mental 'maps' are never made directly from relations with the THINGS, BEINGS, and/or SITUATIONS of EXISTENCE.

The mind needs flexibility to function well. Treating the mind's primary (cognitive) function as that of making ever changing and malleable mental 'maps' is the surest way to establish an appropriate approach to using the mind. To take on such an approach to the functions of mind is to dereify the 'things' of mind. When the mind thus functions more flexibly as a bank for mental 'things' (maps, thoughts, words, definitions, concepts, descriptions, stories, etc.) our BEING is better able to do the ground work for ever more dereification, for ever more liberating spiritual mastery. As one's managements become more supple and lithe, as such managements work to dereify the 'things' of mind, one's BEING is led to its own actualization. Thus, dereification is a wonderful and direct process for reorganizing the functions of mind so to generate greater mental flexibility... which ultimately leads, most gratifyingly, to the achievement of BEING-actualization, of being one's fullest, most extensive BEING beyond all the once believed contrivances of mind.

Planting, cultivating, and nurturing the above seed-formulas (or any variant, thereof) will lead one to BEING-actualization, to being fully one's BEING, to being all-HERE. By the way, when a seed-formula is used with a form of meditation, one has a powerful combination for eventually achieving BEING-actualization.

►**Practicing forms of meditation**
facilitates passing through these 'worlds' of words,
so to arrive, unbeworded, HERE in this WORLD.

...

The basic concept underlying the precept "**the**
'thought' is not the THING" is found throughout
history, in one form or another. One can find its
likeness in Eastern philosophies; and, in the West, one
finds it predominantly in the philosophical-
phenomenological tenets underlying the sciences,
whereby, all thought is treated as "hypothesis" [a kind
of symbolic mental 'map']. A hypothesis is, of course,
a thought that is understood to be no more than a
symbolic representation of some 'thing' <u>indirectly</u>
derived from some THING or THINGS in pure-
EXISTENCE. A thought, a mental 'thing,' is no more
than a symbolic or hypothetical representation, a
'map', derived from <u>some mental data</u>, themselves,
derived from the perceptions of the senses meandering
through some TERRITORY to which some thinker is
exposed—some thinker like you or me.

All of the variations of the original primary precept,
"**the 'thought' is <u>not</u> the THING**", act as seed-
formulas for major change with respect to how one's
BEING relates to mind. As mentioned, they all can
open to BEING-actualization.

54

Here follows another important variation of the above seed formula. Much of the "wisdom" of the long-lived quest for spiritual liberation can be reduced to this formula:

"Our BEING is <u>not</u> thinkable."

A Beneficial Side-Effect

By the way, as you may have discerned, this manual is predominantly about <u>how to be</u> and only secondarily about <u>how to do</u>. <u>Without</u> our BEING being well-grounded in ITS BEINGNESS, often enough, <u>doing</u> can have detrimental results, can be comparable to the spinning of wheels that take us no where new, or can cause us to act from false or inappropriate 'maps', 'maps' that can even cause us to be violent towards our fellow BEINGS.

Although it is not a primary goal of this manual, <u>doing well</u>—achieving high mental performance—is a beneficial side-effect of being fully one's BEING, of being all-HERE. When one clears one's mind of the sundry, unnecessary bits (bytes) of baggage that rest upon it like an overburdened burro, one finds one's BEING more able to lithely apply the mind to tasks and problems of practical, concrete, every-day living. This de-burdening is equivalent to increasing one's proficiency and, thus, intelligence—in other words, to becoming a more effective doer. This de-burdening refs again to the process of dereification (de-reification).

The mind that is flexible in its ability to make alternative 'maps' (representational abstractions or structures) is one that cultivates intelligence. In that the mental dysfunction of reification is the process of treating the abstract 'things' of thought as though they were equivalent to or associated with the notion called "reality"—some 'thing' that has no alternatives, reification is a major cause for making the mind's functions less flexible and intellectually rigid.

When a rigid approach to reified 'things' is obviated by recognizing that the 'things' are best approached as being provisional structures of symbols, when our mental 'maps' are recognized as never equivalent to any THING or BEING of pure-EXISTENCE, then, the thinker can more easily go—with greater proficiency and intelligence—from thought to thought, from mental 'map' to mental 'map'. Thus, another phrase for this process of increasing the facility for going from 'map'-to-'map', of increasing one's intelligence, is to engage in "a process of removing the mind's reifications". Thus, dereification increases intelligence.

▶Dereification makes the mind more flexible; thus, it increases intelligence.

As we dereify the 'things' of our minds, so to manage them as the symbolic structures they truly are, we come that much closer to having the intelligence for seeing a mind's 'universe' for what it is, a big mind-made 'thing', which, in the long-run, makes it that much easier to step out of the rigid matrix of a mind into the pure, unadulterated, indescribable, flowing, and completely dereified HERE—this HERE wherein we have the benefit of being actualized BEINGS. Allow me to add, being all-HERE makes one's life a lot easier to manage and, ultimately, more satisfying.

Dereification offers the above beneficial side-effects. However, working with or improving intelligence is somewhat outside the purview of this manual. It is not designed to offer elaborate methods or programs for helping to take advantage of a new-found clarity. It is just meant to bring one there, and thus, HERE.

However, some help in the practical management of the mind's 'things' is offered in a companion book, The Handbook of BEING. Even without such help, this new found clarity naturally provides its own new approaches and useful methods for not getting caught in old rigid habits and mental traps that slow thinking down and, in some cases, stop it, altogether. Dereifying one's mental structures goes hand and hand with increasing flexibility in the management of cognitive structures. Thus, for the liberated or actualized BEING, management of the mind becomes progressively easier as a result of greater proficiency in thinking with dereified 'things'.

Each individual has her/his own unique or singular pattern of interests. As a fully actualized BEING, one naturally and consciously develops her/his own symbolic mechanisms for dealing with such interests. Thereby, each develops or generates her/his own approaches to working and reworking the verbal, visual, perceptual-conceptual structures of a well-functioning, well-managed, fully dereified mind (a well-self-programmed biocomputer).

Let's Take a Closer Look

As the multi-sensory inputs, percepts, and imageries of the mind interact with the filters provided by the mind's cognitions and memories, they produce virtual 'things' for us to use for negotiating the byways of LIFE and EXISTENCE. An image in the mind is—by virtue of its own representational nature—a virtual 'thing'. As we touch the THINGS of the WORLD with our senses, each touch makes for a recognizable incident of the virtual—the mind's multi-sensory imagery. Hence, our lives are experienced and lived in virtual-being. At this point, the important issue to address is "what are we to do as BEINGS within the conditions of such naturally imposed virtual-being?" Are we going to treat its contents as "real" or are we going to manage it for the symbolic, representational structures that it contains?

All in all, it is only via awareness—of the fact that all perception and thinking produces virtual-being—that we have a chance to adequately manage the mechanisms of the mind for further ongoing well-being and survival. As mentioned, herein, the best way of doing that is via the means of using the modus of symbolic thinking which is exemplified so well in the scientific method. [Much more on how to use this method for safe, sound, and sane mental management is presented in other well-written books on this subject and, more specifically, in the Handbook of BEING.]

Okay. If our lives are of virtual-being and we too frequently suffer from not knowing this, just how are they virtual? And, secondly, if then "virtual", how can we help ourselves become aware of the virtual aspects of our minds' productions; i.e., how can we be BEINGS while dereifying the all-too-often believed (reified) 'things' of mind, i.e., how can we come to live, function, and manage more fully and authentically?

This manual attempts to address these questions. The first question gives purpose to this manual and the second question is meant to bring forth a solution. For *spacenow*, I'll give a somewhat truncated answer to the second question:

By learning that we are non-virtual BEINGS who use virtual-systems to survive in a non-virtual WORLD.

-or-

By dereifying the 'things' of mind which brings one to being all-HERE, to BEING-actualization.

If you think that your way of *seeing* your life, of being a "civilized person", is to some extent not authentic—that it is, in effect, too consumed by the "virtual", then the task for this author will be immensely easier... easier, because you may, in fact, already be on a way to being fully your non-virtual BEING, all-HERE. This can be the case regardless of the fact that the products of mind are, per necessity, composing theaters of virtual-being.

However we look at it, our task of getting our BEING to fully reject or repudiate any inappropriate relations between our BEING and the mind is a worthwhile and rewarding endeavor; for, via such rejection/repudiation we come to eliminate the matrix-prison (that the mind can so readily construct) and, by so doing, become the actualized BEING that is our original birthright.

We should take note that, if we do not come to eliminate these "prisons for our minds", we will just keep on believing our virtual 'worlds' to be <u>identical</u> to the otherwise holistic, interdependent, non-conceptual, and non-virtual WORLD within which we truly live and still exist. As painful as inauthentic living can be, there is something worse awaiting us, so-called *humans*, as a result of our living inauthentically. There is the collapse of those LIVING-SYSTEMS that give foundation to our civil structures. Inauthentic living causes us to lose contact with those living mechanisms that, otherwise, aid us in our long-term endeavor to survive as a species.

▶ **For sentient BEINGS, inauthentic living is the precursor to civil and ecological collapse.**

This manual is for those who would like to live authentically, for those who would prefer to live this lifetime as fully as possible—as the fullest incarnation, manifestation, substantiation, materialization, and spiritualization of our BEING as possible. This manual is for those who would free their BEING from the prisons (those built within the believed limits of personal matrices), for those who would have a guide on how to achieve (simply and relatively easily) the ongoing PROCESS of BEING-actualization.

We can stand upon the earth of our planet as unadulterated and verbally unsullied BEINGS.

Its Own 'Universe'

▶ **A mind's 'universe' cannot capture the pure-EXISTENCE of the SPACE about us.**

The mind is its own 'universe' and each belongs to its keeper. In other words, as a mind filters EXISTENCE it makes a personal 'universe' (or 'world'). This seems so obvious, but, then, why do so many people act as though they do not know this... and, then, of course, *think* they know it all? Apparently, it is not so obvious.

So, here's the rub: if we do not always remember that these unique 'universes' or 'worlds' function only as collections of operationally-working virtual 'maps', i.e., as <u>creations or generations</u> of mind, we tend to dysfunction as thinkers, often, miserably so. So miserably, we cannot stop ourselves from committing those forms of mass-murder called "genocide" or "war". Personally, I was born on the edge of what was called a "World War" in which some 55 million people were murdered—all for good reasons, of course. Since my birth, humans have committed one war upon another. The ability to reify BEINGS into 'enemy' is a sickness of the mind. Today, we appreciate that the biologies of the oceans are being directly (in the case of 'food') or indirectly (in the case of 'waste' or 'effluent') "murdered". This sickness must be cured or we, as a species, along with a great number of our fellow BEINGS, will meet our end. [At this moment, the Earth is suffering from a mass extinction called the Anthropocene Extinction.]

At best, one's 'universe' has some useful representational value. At worst, it causes dysfunctions that shape neurosis or psychosis for the unsuspecting word-user who believes the beworded 'things' of mind. This is so, **because the word-believing word-user is unable to adequately challenge the presumptions of thought** and, hence, is unable to establish a proper relationship with the arbitrarily believed and misleading persuasions of mind. [Just ask anyone who has survived a mental illness.]

While working on its own 'universe', a mind can only process its own symbols and models, its own mental 'maps', of EXISTENCE... nothing more. It is to play with the elements of poor thinking or, even, of insanity to assume or pretend that a symbol can have "real" standing. As a fine example, we see how millions of humans confuse their mental symbols with the ULTIMATE GROUND of EXISTENCE. Thus, we have words like 'dios', 'god', 'allah' that have become mental "idols" for many an unsuspecting word-believer; whereby, such words with their descriptions are confused with the ultimate THING-IN-ITSELF, whatever IT is. By the way, idols do not come in the form of external objects, like "golden calves" are imagined to do; rather, idols exist only in the mind, internally, as believed mental 'things'. We cannot deny the miraculous of the first apparition of the "something from nothing", of the first THING from the Void. However, we can deny the validity of 'what' the mind does with IT, as it tries to understand the miraculous. To assume the mind's names, attributions, and description to be equivalent to the ULTIMATE is to commit a form of confusion called "idolatry". Found even in doctrinal thinking, it is simply a very poor way to manage the mental maps of the mind. [This latter insight seems too subtle for many to appreciate.]

This previous example demonstrates how many of this planet's religions cause their "flocks" to reify the 'things' of mind. In many a religion, we see how humans raise symbols to the pedestal of the notion "reality". Although religions are constantly inventing 'things' to project them onto EXISTENCE, even so, at more sophisticated levels of thinking, they do occasionally deal with such reifications by referring to them as "idols". Yet, it seems that most frequently they are unable to appreciate how using words to give description to the ULTIMATE-THING-IN-ITSELF is also an act of "idolatry". To worship some 'thing' of the mind is to practice idolatry. If one looks closely enough, one sees that nearly all religions are based upon a grand idolatry of verbal constructs.

Curiously, the practice of idolatry is considered to be a "sin", to be "sinful". If 'sin' were not just another projected concept of a certain kind of absolutistic (non-relativistic) thinking, it would, indeed, be "sinful". Yet, in that sin exists only because some human invented the idea or concept of 'sin', we may readily say that it is "not sinful", but, that it is merely "poor thinking" or, occasionally, "insane thinking" to approach symbols as though they could transplant any THING-IN-ITSELF! All the wars, religious wars, genocides, and, even, the human-made ecological collapses of Earth's history are due to being unable to appreciate the THINGS, BEINGS, and LIVING-SYSTEMS of BEINGS beyond the utilities of the believed mental 'maps' that transplant THEM. For ongoing examples of such confusion, we see how we are allowing terms like 'enemy', 'terrorist', and 'food' to rob us of those due-processes of reason and sanity that otherwise prevent such unconscionable occupations and exploitations that lead to violence, war, genocide, and ecological destruction. As an exemplary case, we see how populations of BEINGS are being decimated as 'food' ("fish"), how THEY are removed from the waters, from the oceans and seas.

When we "suffer" from the delusion that our thoughts are more than 'maps'—that they might have some "absolute" quality about them, we are then teetering upon the brink of neurosis, often leading to psychosis. To maintain one's BEING in modes of sanity, of valid, easy functionality, the BEING must never be fooled into thinking that the mind's products are any more valid than arbitrary mental 'maps', provisionally employed as useful symbolic representations.

And, here's another rub: <u>Way too few humans have even an inkling that their thoughts are only symbolizations</u>. They do not appreciate that the thoughts of their minds (biocomputers) are only 'maps' built from sensory-cognitive data and, therefore, can <u>never be equivalent to pure, unadulterated EXISTENCE</u>. [The educators of this planet have their work ahead of them!]

Believing thoughts to be equivalent to pure-EXISTENCE causes one to not question one's personal mind-made 'maps'—thus, by so believing, one goes about forming the personal foundations of one's own rigid and inflexible thinking, ultimately, one's own matrix—which, as suggested above, can cause all kinds of dysfunction, from neurosis/psychosis to civil warring, genocide, and ecological disaster.

If we do not question, we lose the ability to adapt to changing circumstances, to a change-filled WORLD, to a WORLD that needs our flexible stewardship.

► **In essence, it can be said that <u>to so believe</u> is to stop thinking.**

For, thinking is not about rehearsing old mental files. It is about managing new information and revamping the old in order to negotiate an ever-changing WORLD.

As defined, herein, a <u>mental matrix</u> is fashioned by the <u>unconscious notion</u> (knowtion) that the 'maps' of mind are, to varying degrees and in varying circumstances, <u>equivalent</u> to pure-EXISTENCE. When one supposes that one has "reality" in the mind, one need not think. Thus, thinking ultimately stops for the true-word-believer captured and influenced by the reified 'things' of one's own matrix, one's own *believed* mental theater. [To some extent tongue-in-cheek, are these not the symptoms of some kind of catatonia?] Yet, to a great extent, the mental dysfunctions of humanity are indeed due to that form of belief referred to, herein, as "reification".

Unfortunately, it is very easy for us word-users to be unconscious of those 'things' that block consciousness. Often, we are only <u>potentially</u> conscious BEINGS. It should be obvious that for those *humans* who are not aware of that which aids consciousness, things like mental acuity, full maturity, sanity, and, ultimately, BEING-actualization can only remain dim mirages, alien to one's everyday functioning.

Herein, in terms hopefully accessible to many readers, we are exploring the tools and ways of mind, so to achieve, eventually, an appropriate relationship with that pure BEING that is and must ever be recognized as being the source of unobstructed consciousness. We especially must recognize that a consciousness of our BEING, of pure-EXISTENCE, of LIFE, of ALL that is right HERE, is made possible by going beyond the reified 'things' of mind—most notably, beyond all these noisetools—to a recognition that all THINGS and BEINGS are never captured by any mind-made 'things'.

►**Consciousness is made possible by going beyond the 'things' of mind to a recognition that no 'thing' captures any THING.**

'Worlds' of Words

Words ("noisetools") are essentially tools that have specific utility and, most importantly, <u>significant limitation</u>. As tools they cannot do more than offer arbitrary representations of the 'stuff' of mind. Noisetools (words) are but mental 'things' and, as such, should not be assumed to give more than incidentally personal, thinking-system-dependent, representation to one's sensory "experience". Predominantly, noisetools help construct and bind mental 'maps'. We only fool ourselves when we assume they bind pure-EXISTENCE or our ineffable BEINGNESS. To function as though they do or could do that is to <u>dysfunction</u> in the use of language and in the management of the thought-up, beworded 'things'.

We hardly give it its due, but we humans are born into 'worlds' of "words", like fish into water. And, like fish in water, we are immersed in the habits of language and (most often) are not aware of either the medium or the habits we acquire. For not having another medium to which to compare, most fish are surely unaware of water, yet, it is water that carries all of their actions into play. So it is with humans, with regard to language and the language-filled mind.

If we liken the mind to a machine that makes 3-d, moving images (clips or series of 3-dimensional structures) from sensory data—all somewhat removed from EXISTENCE—then words or noisetools are the mortar that helps to hold those structures together. As such, these mind-made 'things' are, for the thinker, supporting the <u>virtual nature</u> of the other 'things' of mind. Thus, words are what name and interconnect virtual 'things'. Moreover, with a little <u>poor</u> education, words become the means for labeling and fixing those structures into static reifications. As labels, the arbitrary or incidental application of words tends to perpetuate the reifying processes of human thought.

►Human <u>thinking</u> is shaped by the powerful medium of language.

Obviously, human language is superimposed upon the already virtual imagery of the mind. And, <u>human actions</u>, in themselves, are then shaped by human thoughts to fulfill human purposes, intentions, and utilities. Of course, the container for all this is what we call the "mind". The serious flaw in all this is apparent as we notice how easy it is to cause thinking to suffer from the inflexible tendencies of reification. This is why we humans must find the volition for educating ourselves and our children about the necessary processes of dereification.

Thus, achieving a proper relationship to mind is all-important. For, by so doing we are able to achieve proficiency in using and managing the mind for the long-term well-being of our lives. As that which leads us to actualizing ourselves as BEINGS and to sustaining ourselves as BEINGS among BEINGS, this proper relationship must be a primary concern. As *human beings* who would live good lives—lives that would provide adequate understanding and self-assurance for our children, we must give ourselves the tools that would allow us to manage our 'worlds', so to fulfill ourselves as BEINGS who live in a vast

COMMUNITY of BEING, in the BIOSPHERE of a LIVING-WORLD.

▶ **We live in 'worlds' of assembled words that are <u>not</u>, in themselves, able to be equivalent to the WORLD about us.**

Unfortunately, as we live in such 'worlds', we tend to become increasingly isolated from the WORLD; we tend to be unaware that there are living, biologically interdependent, and wondrous LIVING-SYSTEMS about us!

So, we are fooled! And, as each such 'world' devolves into being a separate matrix, we are contained, divided and conquered, and spiritually-intellectually defeated.

The TERRITORY of BEING

▶ **The TERRITORY of BEING is always right "HERE".**

**Disillusionment is good.
No one should live in a 'world' of illusions.**

To free one's BEING from the illusions of a personal matrix one need only step out of it... into being all-HERE. Of course, for those who are owned by a personal matrix (in varying degrees and circumstances) to step-out is not, necessarily, so easy.

70

In the East, long ago, schools were established, in monasteries (etc.), with that one final step in mind. To step out of the Grand Illusion, out of the "maya" of mind, was seen to be the most important step that a young person could make towards a mastery and maturity of mind and living. In the East, they call this Grand Illusion "maya". As a consequence of a well-received movie, I am using the term "matrix" with the hope that it will be a popular synonym for "maya". There is a need for a broadly popularized term that can give expression to how believing the beworded, reified, 'things' of mind can keep us mentally imprisoned. We may hope that a well-received neologism (Neo-logism) that defines the mechanisms and structure of the "prison for your mind" may help free more of us to be HERE in the simple glory of LIFE and BEING.

▶ **Matrix = Maya**

The Importance of Repetition

Throughout this manual major concepts are repeated with respect to the varying subjects and circumstances discussed. I am trying to adequately present a major underlying precept (**"The 'thought' is <u>not</u> the THING."**) with the hope that the reader may see how it affects a great variety of "fields" of thought, thus, to instill and reinforce the experience of viewing <u>thinking</u> in terms of it being only the <u>processing of mental 'maps' or dereified symbolic structures</u>.

►**To think is to process symbolic structures.**

[Remember, as symbols are only symbols, mental 'things' are only 'things', 'maps' are only 'maps' and thoughts are only thoughts.]

For many of us, to think symbolically is not habitual; therefore, practice and repetition to get it to be habitual are necessary. As a manual, this book should be read and reread in short takes, to be chewed, mulled over, pondered, researched, walked and slept with. It is one thing to have a good idea. It is another to practice it, to internalize it, and to apply it to our lives.

If the reader were a child and her/his course and courses of living were permeated with an understanding of how thoughts are first and foremost symbolic representations, only maps of mind, this manual would not be necessary, and, its repetitions not called for. Instead the child in us is too often fed and trained by systemic indoctrinations—those of old language and static society—all marshaling towards the inappropriate process of confusing pure-EXISTENCE with old and often looping 'thoughts'. For such indoctrinations, we tend to believe the TERRITORY of pure-EXISTENCE to be <u>equivalent</u> to the 'maps' of mind. Just how appropriate is it that we should turn our BEING over to believing that we can be identified merely as 'things' of mind; how appropriate is it for us to allow our BEING to be divided into different groups of word-believers who end up being controlled by those who would manipulate words so to maintain personal power <u>over</u> our BEING? How appropriate is it to allow ourselves to be divided up into "blacks", "reds", "whites", "yellows", etc? These are rhetorical questions that point out how we lose our spiritual-intellectual freedom and integrity to the tyrannies of words that develop as we are indoctrinated into being unable to see how the beworded 'things' of mind are recognized as being merely the virtual, symbolic 'maps' of mind.

Ever since the beginnings of language, there has been no more powerful a mechanism for power and control than to have people believe words! Just look at how the mere mention of the name of one god or another has made it possible for whole armies of ignorant humans to go to the killing fields to slaughter each other for those who would speak for the gods, for those who would have us believe that some families have divine rights over others, for those who would not have us come to appreciate that all words are but arbitrarily and incidentally conceived symbols, mind-made 'maps', for those who stand to gain from our ignorance. How appropriate is it for us BEINGS to give our wondrous BEINGNESS over to those who use words to maintain power and control over us?

A little repetition of a liberating formula can help us BEINGS to see just how naïve it is to allow the belief-in-words to blind us to how the beworded 'things' of mind divide us into separate groups, gangs, armies, troops, parties, races, religions, cults, congregations, cliques, bordered countries, (etc.) that so easily maintain power over our otherwise unified, individually free, and loving BEING.

Depending upon where one is at, spiritually and psychologically, the repetition herein may feel redundant; however, it is the writer's hope that such repetition will lead to little eureka's, satori's, insights, and epiphanies. No one can say where anyone's at spiritually or intellectually. So, if the repetitions do seem redundant, please, accept them as exercises towards seeing a basic principle applied to a variety of lens and scenarios—perhaps, with the outcome of seeing differently—with new eyes.

The real voyage of discovery consists not in seeing new landscapes, but in having new eyes.

—Marcel Proust

Managing In LIFE

Living is ultimately quite simple. Notwithstanding, the theaters of language and thought lead the wayward BEING to invent for ITSELF all kinds of complexity, all kinds of quandaries, all kinds of tragedy. Much of this complexity is produced by the BEING getting entangled in the unnecessarily complex scripts, the believed or reified programs, of mind. What a study it is to investigate just a few of the fixed programs, thought-systems, belief-systems, the mental constructs and paradigms, the conundrums, enigmas, and vicious circles that some minds are able to generate. Such study is interesting and challenging, however, from this author's viewpoint, the discomfort, misfortune, and bereavement that often accompanies an ordinary thought-system, a typical belief-system, causes one to see this theater as more so ironically "sad and tragic" rather than just "interesting".

People like Hitler, Stalin and other famous maniacs of incredibly nefarious matrices were especially good at *thinking* their thoughts equivalent to pure-EXISTENCE, to the greater TERRITORY. Their actions spoke loudly of their reified thoughts.

Our WORLD is filled with examples of reified outlooks and paradigms that show how not being aware of the symbolic nature of our invented thoughts can cause the murder of millions upon millions of innocent BEINGS, BEINGS who are always the "collateral damage" resulting from believed 'things' held in the minds of those who are unable to see beyond them! The term 'collateral damage' is, itself, just another obscene reification that permits some people to say that their own objectives are more important than the lives of those BEINGS who get in the way of their priorities and actions, actions which are already filled with murderous intent. Some people truly do not know what they do!

►We have our minds; we need not be had by them.

The Issues of a Manual

Now that the essential considerations of this manual are introduced, especially, the primary precept: "the 'thought' is not the THING" [with its synonymous variations], it behooves us to review the issues of this manual. They are presented as questions:

What is entailed in being a BEING?

What roles do language and the language-filled mind have with respect to preventing our BEING from actualizing ITSELF and from being all-HERE?

How is our BEING prevented from managing the mind (biocomputer) with all its images and words so to maintain an attitude of "healthy indifference" for the functions of mind?

What steps are required so that we may actualize as BEINGS, so to free our BEING from the thought-up prison that the mind so readily makes, so to come to experience the ordinary joys of being fully in and of the flows of LIFE?

What is required to improve our lives with respect to being entirely HERE on this planet of interconnected, living, ecological systems— thereby, to come to appreciate how our personal

BEING is an extension of an all-inclusive, interdependent WHOLE, a global system of precious living-ecologies?

> [Again, this last issue has an associated thesis published in the Appendix: The Reification-Extinction Thesis.]

By the way, there is a very small number of apparently well-meaning people on this planet who would turn this planet into a great market place for the consumption of 'things' that require seeing every THING and BEING as resources for the production of such 'things'.

Just thought I'd mention it.

The SEER Ever Remains Unseen

▶ **The eye cannot see THAT which is doing the seeing, so our BEING cannot see ITSELF.**

Our BEING uses the mind to make mental images and it is those images that compose seeing. As the SEER that does the seeing, as the EYE of consciousness that *sees*, our BEING is unable to actually *see* ITSELF, THAT which is doing the seeing.

When you would *see* some THING or some BEING, you are seeing a virtual 'thing' in the back of your brain. You come closest to *truly seeing* THEM when you receive the data of your senses without giving labels, descriptions, and mind-made interpretations to the images.

►**Our conscious BEING is the SEER,
never 'the seen'!**

The THINKER Ever Remains Unthought

►**The mind cannot think THAT which is doing the thinking, so our BEING cannot think ITSELF.**

As we see <u>only</u> images in the mind, in like manner, our BEING, as the THINKER, thinks <u>only</u> with imagined 'things' of mind. **Our thoughts are only 'things' of mind.** When our BEING thinks of ITSELF, IT does so with virtual 'things' within a mind-made 'world' of virtual-being. When we take these 'things' as able to stand for WHO we are, we are seriously fooling ourselves while laying the foundations for mental prisons to which we sentence our own BEING, often enough <u>for life</u>, to a life of artificial suffering that feels ever so "real".

►**In that our thoughts are never more than 'things' of mind, we are never able to truly *think* our own BEING.**

The fact that the THINKER cannot *think* ITSELF into the 'things' of mind without making ITSELF a prisoner of mind brings us back to one of the corollaries of the main precept of this manual, to that singularly most simple and effectively most useful principle for achieving BEING-actualization:

78

▶ **Our BEING is <u>not</u> thinkable.**

We can think 'things' about the manifestations of our minds, about what we do as BEINGS. Yet, we can never *think* our BEING! A thorough understanding of this seed-formula makes it possible for our BEING to actualize ITSELF as fully, actually, and actively all-HERE.

How we think and act depends upon the makeup of an ever personal virtual 'world', a grand-structure of mind-made, virtual 'things'. And, every one of us carries such a virtual 'world' about. Unless we can free our BEING from believing the 'things' of these 'worlds', we can only remain as *humans* who treat ourselves and each the "other" according the incidental characteristics, qualities, features, and dispositions of relatively fixed structures, structures that are not appreciated for their artificiality. In other words, as long as we do not appreciate that the mind makes virtual-being, we are all at the mercy of our own and each other's arbitrary mind-made 'things', 'things' that will be, often enough, unpredictable, irrational, unreasonable, unfair, capricious, and unjustified.

When we can no longer behold the BEING beyond our mental 'worlds' and, consequently, there is no mercy therein, we have "violence" and "war". Moreover, when the grand-structure of an individual gets "in power", where there are few-to-no checks to such power, the arbitrary nature of such a structure easily makes for absolutistic, autocratic, dictatorial, despotic, tyrannical, and unrestrained expressions of will, of which violence and war are typical. [Is there any wonder why educational and political systems must be democratic?]

Know Not Thyself

The "knowtion" that one can "know thyself" is fraught with inconsistency. If taken literally, the idea that our BEING can *know* ITSELF is even foolhardy and dangerous. At best one can recognize that one is HERE; but, it is counterproductive to the well-being and sanity of our BEING to try to assume that we can squeeze IT into the 'things' of mind, which is, after all, what it means literally to *know* something.

With regard to the greater BEINGNESS that permeates the ecologies of our planet, it is the assumption that we *know* the THINGS of our WORLD that is causing the current Anthropocene Extinction. The ecological sustainability of a planet is being undermined by 'what' the typical human *knows*. In some areas of LIFE, it is by far better to be in awe of THINGS than to assume we *know* THEM. When we *think* we *know*, we often stop holding THINGS and BEINGS in reverence.

▶Woe are we when we think we *know* our BEING.

The "EYE" of consciousness constitutes our BEING's awareness; but, as the EYE cannot *see* THAT which is doing the seeing, so our BEING cannot *know* THAT which emanates or generates its own consciousness.

Although we can feel, *see*, and detect the manifestations our BEING, which proves and convinces us that we are, THAT which is doing the feeling, *seeing*, and detecting is not ITSELF contained by the impressions of these processes.

▶ **We can consciously feel our BEING; but, we can never *know* our BEING.**

Our BEING can never be squeezed into the virtual 'things' of mind. Thus, we discover the awe and reverence that permits us to steward our BEING and the BEINGNESS of our WORLD.

▶ **To our unthinkable BEING we are to be true.**

Under the influences of the word-filled mind, our BEING can imagine that IT is thinking of ITSELF. Yet, when this happens, we our merely projecting mental 'maps'—mind-made, verbally emphasized structures—unto our BEING. Such 'maps' or mental 'things' have arisen from the specific linguistic and cultural experiences and persuasions to which one's BEING has been exposed. "Am I truly a white man or a black man?" The fact is that such a 'thought' can no more enclose the BEING-THINKER than can the images in the back of the brain <u>contain</u> the SEER who sees and contemplates those images.

▶ **Our BEING is never equivalent to the symbols, 'maps', or screenings of mind!**

►One can come to manage one's thoughts; however, no one can ever come to *see* or to *think* one's BEING; for all thoughts are merely 'things' of mind.

By trying to *see*, *find*, *think*, or *know* the BEING, we are putting the mind onto an impossible task. We are asking the mind to equate its 'things' with our truly unthinkable BEING. We are engaging it in an endless subprogram that can be well described as just another endlessly looping "virus" of the softwares of mind, just another biocomputer virus.

►As we equate our BEING to 'things', we are making mental viruses for the biocomputer.

As long as such viruses occupy the mind, our BEING will be preoccupied with old mind-made subprograms that cause our attention to loop and re-loop through well-worn patterns, often leading to fatalistic desperation. Often enough, a person so caught will seek escape in any way available, not to exclude those means provided by drugs or even suicide. However, the BEING can free ITSELF from such viruses by simply recognizing that they are, after all, only fictional contrivances that we have allowed ourselves to believe, thus, to accept as "real".

Regardless of the haphazard experiences of our lives, our true BEING is not 'what' we think IT into being! Thereby, we can stop looking for a 'solution'—to our spiritual imprisonment and discomfort—in the verbal subprograms of mind. We can recognize that the key comes as we free our BEING from holding on to any of the artificial 'things' of mind. The only true "solution" comes as we hold onto our unthought, unadulterated, and extensive BEING—this ever so extensive WHOLE that contains the miraculous LIFE we have always been!

We are not of the naming, labeling, and describing that the word-filled mind mistakenly projects upon our BEING. When the BEING attaches ITSELF to a mental 'map' that pretends to define the BEING in anyway, the BEING is stuck to, bogged down upon, such a 'map'. As stipulated, the verbal subprograms of words and beworded images—of such 'maps'—can only cause one's thoughts to loop about; and so, we have the makings for a biocomputer virus... and, of course, for that kind of shut-down that is so commonly called a "neurosis" or "psychosis". Such viruses are epidemic in our 'worlds' of thought. They are causing a rampant "dys-ease" in all these cultures that tend to reify their own processes of thinking.

▶The BEING is the MAPPER, never the 'map'.

As we come to appreciate that the 'maps' of mind are never able to hold the TERRITORY of any of our BEING, we actualize that our personal 'maps' serve us best when they function as a fluid interface between our "inner" BEING and our extensive "outer" BEING which is coextensive with the greater TERRITORIES of pure-EXISTENCE. At best, our mapping serves to map provisionally the personal data that arrives from sensing the actions and interactions that occur between our BEING and those TERRITORIES. At best, as we use the mind, we appreciate that no TERRITORY should ever be confused with the 'maps' drawn in the mind. In this way, we are able to keep our personal BEINGS ever open to beholding the greater BEING existing beyond the mind.

As to the "inner" BEING and "outer" BEING, we should remind ourselves that such separation exists only because the mind engenders such separation per its own projections. Our "inner" and "outer" BEING remain, in fact, undivided from the interdependent, holistic PROCESSES that constitute LIFE on Earth.

We must ever remember that our BEING can surely map ITS own activities and behaviors, but to map the BEING, ITSELF, is to produce fictions for the often tragically divided ways that our lives play out on the stages of human reifications. Oh! How we continue to believe our extensive BEING into being seen as the 'things' of mind, as merely "other" 'things'! Oh! How we are fooled into treating each the "other" with violence, into murdering and warring upon our fellow BEINGS! Oh! How some of us profit, so misguidedly, from such violence and murder!

Even though our BEING can never actually be fixedly mapped, many of us persistently try to force our BEING onto the singular 'maps'. Ultimately, as too many of us believe our personal 'maps' to have equivalence with our own BEING and other BEINGS, we find our BEING behaving in ways that defeat any attempt to behold IT with awe and reverence. When 'maps' are projected upon our BEING, we are then restricted to the limits or virtual boundaries of those 'maps' (of arbitrary thoughts), to the parameters of our own mind-manufactured 'things'.

BEING-actualization, BEING-fulfillment, becomes possible only when such 'things' are no longer believed and projected. When our minds stop trying to map our BEING, when they stop believing or assuming that the BEING is *thinkable*, they finally become what they should be: conduits between our "internal" BEING and the ever-so extensive BEING lying beyond the mind. When the mind functions in this manner, it allows our BEING to fully actualize ITSELF as contiguous with the first MIRACLE, this ever-present non-conceptual, unthinkable pure-EXISTENCE that ever stands in defiance of the Void. Oh, that some moment, we may all be BEINGS who are joyously HERE, among all this havenly BEINGNESS, in this living MIRACLE in SPACE!

Some 800 years before today's date, a spiritual renegade called "Francesco d'Assisi" had this to say,

**"If you are to be anything in life,
be yourself, and be that to the fullest!"**

—Giovanni di Bernardone

When our BEING finds ITSELF locked into mental programs that sponsor the "belief" that thought-up descriptions, attributions, or definitions can be (consciously or unconsciously) applied to IT, IT can only function in sub-optimal—often dysfunctional—ways. This manual asserts that the majority of the dysfunctions of human living stem from the notion (the *knowtion*) that we can "know" WHAT it is that constitutes our BEING... for that matter, WHAT constitutes LIFE, in general.

▶ **A 'thought' can never be the BEING!**

It is not pleasurable to lose one's mind to the oppressive fixations of <u>believing</u> our BEING equivalent to the language and thought that is directed at our BEING, that language and thought which would impose the screenings of mind onto IT, that is taken as being "real". Oh! How the oppressive fixations of such belief make us <u>prisoners of our own minds</u>! Oh! How we do not see BEINGS blown to bits when they are held to be the 'enemy' or, perhaps, the 'terrorist'! We need to look no farther than the wars of our 'worlds' to see how we do not see the BEING before us! In the future, to the immediate chagrin of those who profit from violence, the people of the WORLD will return violence with concern and empathy for those who are so cut off that they feel they must resort to violence. That is the only way to stop the contagion of violence in the long-run.

▶It is much easier to kill a 'fly' than it is to kill a BEING that flies.

When we are faced with having to participate in war or some other form of genocide, we should ask ourselves about how much easier it is to kill an 'enemy' than it is to kill a fellow BEING who is merely being called "enemy". As we become less naïve about how words are projected upon our BEING, we come to see how some are benefitting by using words in this way. Who is "right" when the manner of how we project our righteous words causes the killing of BEINGS who receive our projections?

BEING-actualization or, as it can be called, BEING-fulfillment, is in fact the result of how we come to a healthy indifference with regard to the projected products of our personal thought-systems. Within the discourses of our lives, there has been and will continue to be a lot of talk about how to better manage these systems. Some of that talk can help significantly towards living a fulfilling life. A lot of it, unfortunately, is just a lot of trumped-up blah, blah, blah that precedes our killing.

Of course, one would hope *humans* may someday get their priorities in line by first actualizing themselves as wondrous and extensive BEINGS. One can only hope that *humans* will achieve relations with the mind that permit awe and reverence for THAT which constitutes the foundation of LIFE on Earth.

We Can Make this Suggestion

▶ **When thinking about our BEING, do not take the thoughts too seriously.**

By taking such thoughts seriously, we weave nets of believed 'things' that act to capture our BEING. We cannot achieve BEING-fulfillment if we are prisoners of our own minds' reified structures. We cannot step out of such structures into the HERE if we do not have the insight that they are merely virtual illusions, that they are spiritual prisons if and when we believe our own projected words and word-filled thoughts to be equivalent to pure-EXISTENCE.

▶ **The true BEING of these FIELDS of LIFE is not reducible to the networks of human 'thoughts'.**

The above message is <u>not a new one</u>. From time to time, there are new ways of making noises about it. If we study the verbal messages of those we may call the "Great Companions"—those various gurus, artists, poets, philosophers, prophets, buddhas, monks, and even some designated saints—all those who at one time or another stir the spiritual-intellectual alphabet-soup, we find messages that can often be translated into our basic precept:

The 'thought' is not the THING.

or

Our BEING is not thinkable.

We choose our precepts and, then, we diligently apply them as seed-formulas of and for our lives, so to nurture and cultivate the FIELDS from which we reap what we sow. By keeping to the precepts of this manual, we can reap the rewards that allow us to "override" those persuasions that would cause us to try to squeeze our BEING into the beworded 'things', those words and thoughts of the sadly misguided mind. By so doing, we can and do achieve that spiritual-intellectual-psychological liberation praised so highly by the Great Companions... some of whom are mentioned herein.

As we accept these basic precepts as "seed-formulas", so to plant them in our ever fertile and newly expectant minds, that we tend with repetition and practice, we come to grow fine products, like new 'trees of knowledge', that remind us that the THINGS and BEINGS of LIFE are ultimately and wondrously ineffable. To switch metaphors, we appreciate that a good precept can shelter our BEING from the reign of

BEING-defeating thoughts and actions, this by leading us out of believing the 'things', to dereify them all and, thus, to achieving BEING-actualization. By understanding the import of any of the precepts of this manual, we can free ourselves from the matrices of our minds, so to discover the awe, beauty, and joy of fully being BEINGS who are actualized in this unthought, extensive HERE, <u>where all of us are ever present to each the "other" and to all the BEINGS of a LIVING-WORLD</u>.

▶**Step into the HERE to fully behold THEM; and, you will soon actualize how they will fully behold us.**

The 'Worlds' of Some BEINGS

With respect to many a forward-thinking BEING, all 'things' are made in mind and, then, are further filtered by other 'things' of mind. Here is a summary for dealing with our 'worlds':

- Our BEING exists in spite of any 'world' of mind.

- The WORLD about our BEING exists inside and outside of mind.

- With respect to this WORLD, the THINGS and BEINGS of IT are selectively sensed by the mind and, thus, transformed into mental 'things' ("information") that tend to constitute their own mental 'worlds'.

- Shaped from mental data, impressions, images, maps, imaginings, words, and thoughts, our mental 'worlds' induce actions that reflect those 'worlds'. All such 'worlds' and 'things' are incidental generations/creations.

- As a unique system of words, one's culturally influenced language causes the mind to categorize, classify, and index in culturally specific and arbitrary ways. The specific 'things' (the images, thoughts, words, etc.) of an individual's mind must reflect the influences and biases of the language derived from one's personal culture. [The Handbook of BEING focuses more on the mechanics of how we may better manage the influences of language.]

- The proficiency by which we process the 'things' of thought determines the qualities of those 'states' of mind that generate our actions and that, in turn, constitute how we function as individuals in the various times and cultures of this planet.

- Of paramount importance is the fact that **the mind does not** *detect* **'things'** <u>in the</u>

external WORLD. Rather, it **projects** its 'things' onto that WORLD. Thus, the 'worlds' of our minds are virtual projections. Often enough these are <u>unconsciously</u> projected upon the WORLD, with the subsequent potential that the mind would hold a grand mental illusion as equivalent to pure-EXISTENCE. Herein, we are calling this grand illusion a "matrix".

- Thus, how one processes the mind's 'things' determines whether one will be able to see beyond any 'state' of mind to the essential PROCESS of BEING that exists beyond all such 'states'.

- The adverse effects of believing 'states' of mind can easily derail one from effectively allowing for an adequate spiritual-intellectual growth that would lead one to achieving BEING-actualization within this grand COMMUNITY of LIFE and BEING.

The Illusion of Separate 'Parts'

There is this WHOLE-BEING that is greater than the sum of any of ITS mind-made 'parts'.

All these 'parts' (or 'things') are generated by combining the filtered data of our senses with the old conceptions of mind, all derived indirectly from how our definitions of words mix with the imageries of mind. Thus, we have the duty to ever remind ourselves that <u>the mind generates conceptual divisions</u> that make 'parts' of our perceiving and thinking. Such reminding reveals to our BEING that we, ourselves, are not merely 'parts' of any or anyone's mind. It also reveals just how dangerous are those misguided thoughts that would continue to portray our BEING and the BEING of our WORLD as just a collection of so many separate 'things'.

Take heed when you hear BEINGS being <u>deemed</u> to be 'subjects', 'heretics', 'criminals', 'enemies', or 'terrorists' (etc.)! You are hearing how THEY are being robbed of the integrity of their BEINGNESS. You are hearing how BEINGS are made to be seen as mere 'things' of some minds. You are hearing how BEINGS are being set up to be treated with disrespect, summary injustice, and violence... as those who have no rights as BEINGS within the MIRACLE of LIFE! We must remember that all tyrannies, wars, and genocides are based upon how we are fooled into accepting the precious BEINGS of our WORLD as being equivalent to the mere 'things' of some minds.

Basically:

Our extensive BEING exists unadulterated;
yet, the mind projects upon IT 'what' it will.
Our BEING exists independent of mind, in pure-

EXISTENCE; thus, if we are to subsist as BEINGS, we must manage every 'thing' of virtual-being.

How our BEING functions with regard to the "every 'thing' else" depends on how IT approaches the mind. Do our minds contain symbolic 'things', 'maps' that represent filtered data, or do they contain the rigid structures of matrices believed to be "real"? If we do not manage the symbolic 'things', we live in virtual-being that controls us. Take a moment to raise your senses from this manual to see how the beworded 'things' can control you, how your 'world' supplants this WORLD. Look at some THING and give IT a name. See how quickly IT becomes a relatively separate 'it' of the mind.

It is never too late to be fully your BEING by stopping the belief in the 'it's' of mind... by starting to see them as the symbolic (representational, hypothetical) 'things' they are. This much is certain, if we are allowing our minds to treat our own BEING and the BEINGS of this WORLD as 'things', we are sorely fooling ourselves and, by so doing, doing damage to THIS, our WORLD.

If we live merely in the 'worlds' of mind, we cannot live fully; for, all 'worlds' are artificial. Yet, we may ever go forward in this WORLD of ours. Bear in mind, it is much easier to do so if we understand how easy it is to be fooled and, then, to <u>forgive ourselves and other BEINGS</u> for having been trapped in the matrices of mind. Only people—who do not appreciate how we are fooled—go to punishment as a remedy. Only people—who do not understand how to be in this HAVEN—use threats of hells to correct our mistakes. We are not our mistakes! And, if we are not punished, but are shown empathy, compassion, and love, we quickly learn from them... like children learning to walk.

All of us, whether called "citizen", "criminal", "soldier", or "enemy", are BEINGS who will soon come to behold the BEING within ourselves, throughout this living WORLD. We will subsist as we recognize ourselves as "BEINGS" of Earth. We may be confident that this will happen; for, were it not to happen, we will no longer be. All of us are worthy in BEING. All of us can be helped along to make just one step… into being all-HERE.

▶ **Regardless of 'what' we may think, none of us is a separate 'part' outside of the union of BEING.**

A Healthy Indifference

This manual suggests that we must cultivate a certain distance from, a healthy indifference for, the influences of the mind with its products (all just 'parts', 'things'). It is ever so important to have such distance or indifference, so that the reified tools of the unliberated "mind" do not blind us from beholding our own undivided and holistically integrated BEINGNESS. As we actualize in BEING, we come to appreciate the integrity of our BEING, the integral value that all THINGS and BEINGS have with regard to the WHOLE. Without such appreciation, our BEING is led about by reified 'things' that inadvertently make prisons for slaves that cannot function outside of the believed virtual-beingness formed from the definitions of believed images and words. Fortunately, outside of the misguided edicts and persuasions of reified thoughts, thoughts that can only impoverish us spiritually, there are millions of BEINGS who have discovered and are discovering how to actualize their BEINGNESS; and, THESE are all busy helping others to behold WHO and WHAT we truly are, beyond the reified 'things'.

The WORLD is changing! Get on board!

Until the moment of general spiritual liberation, which must soon be, we will work towards a general understanding of how BEINGS are never equivalent to the beworded 'things' of mind. We will forgive the ignorance of those deluded *humans* who will use their 'things' to enslave other BEINGS. Whether physical or mental, the effect of enriching some via the impoverishment of other BEINGS—seen as merely 'things', as merely 'cogs' of the schemes and machines—is enslavement. Those sorry few who believe they can personally own the intellectual, material, and living legacy of a planet of living COMMUNITIES have lost sight of the MIRACLE that is LIFE-in-COMMUNITY. Such personal enrichment can only exploit this COMMUNITY to which we all belong, from which we receive the common bounty belonging to the BEINGS of Earth. Such selective enrichment surely does not sponsor the spiritual or organic well-being of our greater BEING. For the continued ecological glory of these marvelous COMMUNITIES, the ever growing consciousness of millions of actualized BEINGS is quietly and peacefully working to make this planetary satellite sustainable for all of its BEINGS. So that they do not fear WHAT they do not understand, we can only hope that the few will awaken soon enough to enjoy the imminent awakening of the many.

►Even the least of us, even the so-called "bacteria" of our soils, form such COMMUNITIES.

The Innocent Mind

Bless its heart, the mind means well. In its innocent attempts to record, classify, and categorize every 'thing', it just does not know that it should not be trying to force its 'things' onto our BEING. It does not know that it should not be *thinking* its own 'things' able to qualify WHO we are. Yet, it is so easy for this mind, governed by its own classifications and categories, to imagine its 'things' equal to WHO or WHAT our BEING is. Thus, we need to help it away from being fooled into believing it can *know* WHO or WHAT we truly are.

To show how it innocently tries to do just that, we have the following example:

My mind (or someone else's) suggests that I am a human being. [Well, there's another fine kettle of fish.] However, if I am truly interested in being the BEING that I most fully am, I will respond by recognizing that I am not, in fact, a "human being"... for 'human being' is a concept of language and thought, and, "I", I am not, nor have I ever been, a mere concept, a mere idea of any mind. So, in order to keep myself spiritually and psychologically fully my BEING, I will help my mind to establish an appropriate <u>healthy indifference</u> for its own the products by helping it to appreciate that I am no more a 'human being' than am I any other concept of language or thought. Rather, to use words, I am a BEING of a miraculous WORLD of BEINGS... no more, no less.

►**When the mind's structures are "believed", they trap us into *thinking* our BEING into all kinds of mind-made 'things'.**

The WHOLE of Our Extensive-BEING

Where does the BEING find ITS ultimate limits? Does IT stop at what we have classified as 'skin' or, does the LIFE of our BEING find ITSELF to be more extensively beyond such defined limits?

I have come to recognize that I am not what I think. I also recognize that the BEING (that I am) is integral to the LIFE about me—interdependent with the so-called "other" lying beyond my "skin". In fact, that which I may call "other" is more appropriately beheld as a continuation of my own BEING—in other words, as more of the "extensive-BEING of this living WORLD". The BEING that I am is in and of each and every ONE—this ONE that is in unity with this WHOLE which is ITSELF always greater than the sum of any and all of ITS mind-made 'parts'.

Sadly, many of us are not able to see the miraculous EXISTENCE of LIFE in "other"—in every ONE. Many of us find ourselves unable to recognize that the LIFE that is of the least of us is the same LIFE that is of all of us. Yet, this much is a certainty:

► **All LIVING-BEINGS issue from the same ORIGIN regardless of "what" we call THEM.**

Thus, there is only one appropriate "identity" for this BEING to which we belong:

the identify of our BEING with this extensive WHOLE of LIFE.

Any other identity makes for divisions where no such division exists in the pure, unadulterated, indivisibleness of EXISTENCE. In other words, to identify our BEING only with ITS extensive SELF, with ITS own non-thinkable, extensive BEINGNESS, brings us to the fullest identity possible, beyond which there is no greater, separate, mind-made identity, at all! Mind you, such wholesome identity cannot give us big heads; for we are all equal as BEINGS within this WHOLE. Thus, we recognize that...

...the LIFE that is of any of us BEINGS is the same LIFE that is of the "least" of us BEINGS.

This is not just some wishful thinking. This is an empirical principle stemming from the fact that pure-EXISTENCE exists without mind and without mind there are no arbitrarily projected divisions that may cut the WHOLE into 'parts'. Whether the WHOLE is called "the BIOSPHERE" or "our WORLD", ITS LIFE is throughout the same. The separate 'parts', the 'things' of human cognition, the utilities, exploitations, and articles of rampant consumption, are all imposed by mind. Our BEING is not born from these 'parts'. IT is born from the WHOLE. These 'parts' are imposed.

Playing With Abstractions

Here is an expression that plays nicely with the abstractions of language:

Our BEING is the UGE looking at ITSELF.

This expression tends to play with the normal parameters of common terms. It may suggest that we BEINGS—having discovered ourselves to be conscious—are, in effect, the UGE, the ULTIMATE GROUND of EXISTENCE (of SPACE/the UNIVERSE/the MULTIVERSE/etc.) looking at ITSELF.

In the last scene of the movie 2001: A Space Odyssey there is an image that resonates with this thought: an embryonic, childlike consciousness floats in outer space with wide-open eyes taking in the galaxies, stars, and planets. Figuratively, that image potentially well represents our consciousness.

We may savor that image like we might a fine painting. In so doing, however, please, remember how some images can intoxicate the mind. As the mind finds itself free just to be an uncluttered conduit between our inner BEING and our extensive outer BEING (as so conceived), we come to go beyond all images to be, finally, the CHILDREN of SPACE that we truly are… perhaps, somewhat poetically, to echo the above.

In order to establish a proper relationship with mind, in order to be fully one's BEING—by which one can actualize one's original, authentic, unadulterated BEING, one can "keep in mind" that **the mind fulfills its most appropriate purpose by being a self-cleaning conduit between our inner BEING and our**

outer BEING, in effect, by joining us into one holistic BEING.

As the stomach, lungs, heart, and eyes serve us, so the mind may serve to sustain us within the LIFE of our extensive BEING. As a dutiful adjunct to our BEING, the mind does not and cannot encompass our BEING. It cannot do so any more than can the stomach engulf, nor the lungs breath, nor the heart pump, nor the eyes see the RECEIVER of all these services. The EATER, the BREATHER, the PUMPER, the SEER is not retained by any 'thing', by any 'thing' produced and marked by mind. Per principle, we could say that the mind is just a 'part' that has a specific and potentially honorable purpose:

to make—for the RECEIVER—cognitive 'maps' of its own perceived and stored data, all derived indirectly from the concrete WORLD.

The mind makes its 'maps' so that our BEING can negotiate the byways of our WORLD. These 'maps' do not serve us if they replace the vision of our BEING in-this-WORLD with themselves.

▶It is of the utmost importance that such 'maps' do not prevent us and, thus, do not close us off from being entirely in and of this indivisible WORLD!

Obviously, the BEING is not limited **to** the products of mind. And, potentially, IT is not limited **by** those products. The mind with its contents is just another 'part' of the energy-filled, concrete, spiritual-material, synergistic WORLD with which our BEING has continuous intercourse. With all its words and images, the mind is only a 'part' of the BEING. As a 'thing' that is worked and used by the BEING, the mind should be viewed (for purposes of thinking and being) as some 'thing' that the BEING can choose to engage, for specific and, hopefully, practical purposes and tasks, all leading to the well-being of all BEINGS.

▶ **Coincidentally, experiencing the joy of being spiritually liberated is a most practical task.**

However, to firmly reemphasize, if the task is to identify the BEING with a particular 'thing' or to capture the BEING on the 'maps' of words and thoughts, one is setting one's mind and BEING up for frustration, for, as repeatedly mentioned herein, such a task does not, ultimately, lead to sustainable and wholesome results. If one's mind continues to pester the BEING with the particularly impossible and frustrating task of trying to capture the BEING, one need only tell it:

"Thank you, I know you're trying to help, but, please, try to map something that is mappable!".

Of course, if the mind won't stop trying to fixedly map the dynamic BEING that we are, well, then, we may just have to get the noisetools out, again—those that can remind us—so to dereify those presumptuous 'things' that would define us, confine us. For instance, we can get this manual out in order to reread sections of it. We can use meditation to put the <u>noises</u> of the mind in their proper place, as signs indicating the presence of symbolic 'things' that we can manage—whenever we wish—as the 'things' they are. To remind us of WHAT is not of the mind, we can take a good walk into the pristine areas of the natural WORLD (those still surviving the onslaught of human utilities). [We may wish to use one of the convenient devices or tools mentioned in <u>The Handbook of BEING</u>.]

After using any of these tools, our BEING can "reboot" the biocomputer without its troubling viruses and derailing subprograms (it only takes a second), to then go about tasks that do not require one's BEING to be mapped as some 'thing' or combination of 'things'. Most importantly, our mind can take on tasks that would add to the well-being and survival of our extensive BEING in this wondrous, living MIRACLE in SPACE. Any task that adds to the privilege of being alive, any task that helps us to recognize that form of recognition we may call "LOVE" is a worthy task. Any task that may cause us to love the original, unadulterated, and authentic EXISTENCE of our BEING is surely worthy of the doing.

Once again looking at more words, the BEING, to which terms like "spirit", "soul", "psyche", "atman", or "I-am" have been applied, is, ITSELF, not a 'thing' of the mind's conjuring. IT is not definable by language or thought. Like an integrated WHOLE that is greater than the sum of the 'parts', the BEING cannot be qualified or quantified. If one is to be fully one's BEING, s/he must come to fully appreciate HER/HIM/ITSELF as inconceivable, as ineffable. And, by the way, s/he must recognize her/his/its BEING as being intrinsically, ultimately, and consummately worthy, in HER/HIM/ITSELF, as being forever accessible and receivable as a MIRACLE of LIFE... ONE worthy for no other reason than that.

And so, when our inconceivable, undivided, and holistic BEING establishes an appropriate relationship with the 'things' of mind, then IT will have found the will and means to be fully consciously HERE within this MIRACLE.

Obviously, having the mind "indoctrinated" by the traditional, cultural, and verbal persuasions of being *human*, the typical individual has a journey to make— a particularly long one without the kind of guidance available herein. In the East, in those special schools called monasteries, the beginner (the neophyte) has, for centuries, deliberately embarked upon this journey for the express purpose of getting to be of this inconceivable BEING. More recently at last, in the West, we are bringing our spirituality down to earth by systemizing the understandings of the relations of BEING to mind and, then, by making these renewed appreciations available to those who seek "the truth". Remarkably, in terms of words, the truth is that <u>the ultimate TRUTH is beyond the 'things' of mind</u>. The highest goal for a goal-occupied mind is to allow our BEING to pass through it—unscathed and unmarked—so to join "in spirit" the greater TRUTH that surrounds IT. The highest "place" for a BEING to go is a PLACE that is not prestigious; for, it does not belong to the 'things' of mind. Only the mind can think in terms of the prestigious! Yet, regardless, all that the mind may make prestigious is but just another 'thing' next to being in the whole TRUTH of BEING whence comes the joy of living.

▶ **There is no TRUTH in the 'things', nor in owning them. There is TRUTH only in being outside of them, unowned by 'things'.**

Herein, we are acquiring the tools for achieving BEING-actualization. At present, we need simply to bring those tools to the average citizen. For, there are those who still cannot see. There are even those who would prevent BEINGS from acquiring such vision, such actualization—often enough, via force and violence. There are those who are <u>inadvertently</u> helping to cause the extinction of our own species. As a species, we need peace and love to steward the LIVING-SYSTEMS of our planet. Yet, how some humans can use violence with the intention of achieving peace and love <u>is comprehensible</u>.

So, we see how unfortunate are those who are unable to behold the BEING in themselves, in and all around them. We see how they can only see the reified (believed) 'things' of their minds. Of old, these 'things' were given labels like "other" and "enemy" and uncountable millions were slaughtered for such labels. Of new, we are urged to use terms like "terrorist", so that we may more easily kill the labeled 'things' (of our minds), 'things' that belie a recognition of the LIFE that is in and of every ONE, 'things' that deny the LIFE of our own BEING and of all the BEING beyond them!

We reap what we sow!

The Child Is HERE

People have talked of "cosmic consciousness". It could be said that each of us is born as a "cosmic child" and, with a little recognition and help, the child could go on to actualize its BEING as being in union with the cosmos. Within such a union, the child in us would continue to appreciate the cosmic in, of, and about all of LIFE.

I like the idea of the "cosmic child", but, somehow, it rings of the very 'things' that I feel tend to obscure WHAT we, all of us, truly are. It may be said that the cosmic-potential is still within us. But, is that not just another wishful projection that would somehow generate separate distinction for the child or for the child-in-us? As much as I like the idea of being *thought* to be "cosmic", we are not of any word or formula of words. We simply are and are to be simply HERE, yet, ever contently so, merely in this PLACE without "real" descriptions and identities.

►I am of the I-AM and that is ALL there is to IT. We are of the I-AM and that is ALL there is to IT.

With better symbolic managements of our mental 'maps', we can find our 'ways' even beyond delightful words like 'cosmic' to the clarity, simplicity, and equanimity of being a BEING who is simply all-HERE. A 'way' to return from being *thought* "cosmic" is found and followed by simply appreciating that our BEING and all BEING, in-ITSELF, stands without being contained by any words or beworded thoughts offered by that dear contraption we call the "mind".

If you wish to follow the "cosmic child" in you to achieve the spiritual liberation of being a BEING who is all-HERE, do so; but, do so only until that clear moment arrives wherein every THING and every BEING is beheld for WHAT IT is... THIS that stands HERE in-between, before, after, and beyond the *meanings* that your mind is giving to these very words now before you!

The "cosmic child" lives on the 'maps' of mind. But, we live beyond all the attributions of these sticky surfaces–where upon our minds would have us rest were we not aware of how important it is to step off them. When the moment comes, we will stop believing the abstractions that control us; we will dereify the 'things' of mind; we will mature spiritually into being BEINGS who use the 'things' without being used by them.

To be... to simply be, we need only to step off the 'maps' of mind, so to freely actualize WHO or WHAT we are beyond all the 'things' of mind and thought.

As West Continues to Meet East

In the West, many of the tools for achieving spiritual/intellectual liberation have been collected haphazardly in the halls of academe and are only gradually seeping into the mainstream of communal living. As "modern" society becomes more and more familiar with the ideas of science and the liberal arts, especially with the rudimentary premise that all thoughts are but hypotheses of individual or subjective expression, the people of the western persuasions are approaching the common experience of understanding that to think is to process symbolic structures, of making and managing mental 'maps', that cannot identify the pure-EXISTENCE of any THING, no more so than can any symbolic 'thing' actually be the THING or BEING symbolized. For our purposes, this signifies that the mind cannot contain WHO we truly are.

It is not some presumptuous pipe-dream of some utopian theme to imagine such a day, for it is no less than a necessity for the future survival of a language-using "*animal*" to be fully aware of that with which it thinks. As symbol users, without adequate awareness, the eventuality of extinction would be only a matter of <u>when</u>... somewhat off in an unseen "future" where no one remains. If we are to survive we are to develop such awareness. A major boon of being all-HERE, of BEING-actualization, comes to our species as we are freed from believing the abstract 'things' of mind that separate us from the BEINGNESS of LIFE, this in exchange for the management of symbolic structures, of mental 'maps', that can no longer replace the awesome EXISTENCE of LIFE. That boon is our own continued survival as BEINGS of civil customs!

▶ **Being all-HERE is required for long-term survival.**

The journey to be all-HERE does not have to be a long one. It just takes one step, figuratively speaking, out of the believed 'things', off the reified 'maps', of mind. We just need to step out of these rigid structures, into an appreciation of this HERE that has always been ever-present for us, whether we are using or not using our biocomputer.

Being Fully Our BEING, All-HERE

We recall the quote of Giovanni di Bernardone:

If you are to be anything in life, be yourself, and be that to the fullest!

As one who could "talk to the animals"—recognizing all of LIFE's generations, as one who "went naked into the country to build a church to care for the meek and pure of heart", as a rebel who was approaching the Great Unknown, the Great Miracle of Existence, the Ultimate Ground of Existence, with an honorable spiritual-intellectual humility that tried to bypass the political usurpations of authority, Giovanni—like other spiritual reformers—proposes that there is a direct connection to be had with the ultimate WHATEVER, regardless of "whatever" one may care to call IT. Giovanni advises that the most important goal in living should be to be fully one's own BEING, thereby, to fully manifest the intrinsic MIRACLE, the pure, unbesmirched WONDERFULNESS of one's own original, unthought-unthinkable BEING—this BEING in and of us all, this BEING beyond the adulterations and idolatries of human language and thought.

When I was eleven years old, I took the above quote as a guiding motto. Though I did not belong to any organized religion that may claim Giovanni (as Francis of Assisi), my young mind liked the image that he talked to the animals and, especially, that the path to fulfillment came not from the prerogatives of some external commands or dogma, but from the fullest manifestation of one's own ultimate, internal WHATEVER! Obviously, I have come to call this

WHATEVER, "BEING". My journey HERE was significantly aided by the advice of Giovanni's seed-formula.

Giovanni urges us to find and to be "yourself and to be that to the fullest". For a child who was predisposed to looking in the mind for resolutions to questions or quests, I had to slough off quite a few 'selves' like layers of an onion, before, finally one day, it dawned on me that I was out of 'selves'. Ergo, the "self" I sought was not itself to be found in the mind. Next, I appreciated that there could be no incidental, mind-made 'self' (for that matter, any 'thing') that could ever correspond to my true and fullest no-mind SELF, now, to be called my "BEING". Finally, my BEING came to appreciate that IT would never again fall for believing my mind's conjurings able to replace THAT which was now being actualized to the fullest as my nonverbal, inconceivable, extensive BEING, our BEING.

So, to generalize, we can appreciate that one can never be THAT to the fullest until all those 'things', all those conceptual 'selves', are peeled away. As indicated earlier, the mind is innocent. It does not *know* that it is trying to replace a recognition of our unadulterated and nonfinite BEINGNESS with its own limiting, finite 'things'. With this understood, any one of us can refocus the mind to allow our BEING to pass through, so to allow IT to step out of the mind, into the HERE, where our most wondrous and truest SELF survives, where our fullest, most extensive BEING thrives with other BEINGS.

I am thankful to all those who have helped me to actualize my BEING, by offering me seed-formulas and stepping stones on my way to being my fullest BEING, to discovering that in order to be THAT to the fullest, I needed only to step into this PLACE, this HERE, where no 'thing' is able to usurp the prominence of THIS, our own undivided BEING.

Enough with all these words!

…

Perhaps, just a small number more:

Dear reader, I hope that you are all-HERE, as an actualized BEING. Perhaps, you are. Perhaps, you are awake, getting ready to shake your thought-wings, to loosen your shoulders, so to open again on to this SPACE in-between, before, after, and beyond all these 'things' now going through your mind. Either way, I say, "Welcome!"

…

Spacenow!

Let's free our BEING of all this pretentious verbiage.

Let's take that step off the 'maps' of our minds.

Let's be fully our BEING by being all-HERE.

Let's put all 'this' aside, simply to be,

right HERE!

☞

X

...where X marks a 'spot' in the mind and also this
SPOT outside of the mind.

If your mind is not clouded by unnecessary things, this is the best season of your life.

—Wu-Men

Appendix

'Single Quotes' and CAPITAL LETTERS

You will have noticed that I am using some curious conventions in my writing. I feel that it is necessary to emphasize certain words (certain "noisetools") occasionally by either putting single quotation marks ('...') around them or by putting them completely in CAPITAL LETTERS. These conventions help make clear some very important distinctions in how one can use noisetools for thinking and writing. In order to introduce why I use these conventions, I will describe a little scene:

> <<You are sitting by a window and are looking out at a forest of trees. You happen to notice one particular tree because it appears beautiful to you and because it provides a strong wood called "oak". For you, this tree exhibits great utility. Its wood is very useful. In your mind, this tree has certain qualities or attributes that together form <u>your concept </u>of this tree.

As you contemplate the scene beyond your window, all-of-a-sudden, you are struck dumb by the observation that even though this 'tree' has meaning to you, it is derived from some THING that is ever so much more than the image that your mind is now projecting, more than just a mind's 'thing'. You appreciate that the <u>original</u> TREE that you perceived is not ITSELF held by the mind. The original TREE is not your mind's 'tree'; rather, IT is a TREE of non-finite and non-conceptual standing. In fact, in that IT is alive, you wish to think of IT as a "BEING"! The original TREE has its own non-conceptual, unthought BEINGNESS, ONE that certainly stands on ITS own. The fact that the original TREE stands on ITS own in pure EXISTENCE behooves you to let your image of IT stand as well on its own, <u>in your mind</u>. In this way, you come to appreciate that you can have a cleaner RELATIONSHIP with the actual TREE, a RELATIONSHIP that is not influenced by the impediments and stumbling blocks of the projected 'things' of mind, a RELATIONSHIP that allows you to hold the TREE in reverence, reverence that all BEINGS deserve for being wondrously of LIFE. Although your mind may be inclined (for purposes of further thinking) to make a bunch of interconnected mental 'its' out of its own conceived 'tree', you have now discovered a new kind of mental humility and clarity. In fact, you appreciate that you have experienced a shift in consciousness that has made you feel that you belong to some THING that is no less than an ongoing MIRACLE. You call this MIRACLE "LIFE on Earth".

HERE you stand by your window. You are thankful that you were struck dumb and that you became awestruck by the unthought potentials of the original TREE. For, now, you are able to see IT as integral to the FABRIC of LIFE. And, for this vision, you are quickly coming to appreciate that your own BEING is ITSELF no less integral to the FABRIC. For, finally, you are able to behold that the TREE and YOU are both of the same LIFE, of the same extensive BEING, ALL of which exists in an incredible simplicity and purity, beyond all the words, all the beworded conceptualizations, and all the 'things' of mind. >>

[End of scene.]

When I want to emphasize that a noisetool is in fact representing a personal concept of something, a mental portrait about something, I like to put single quotation marks ('...') around it. By putting a noisetool like 'tree' within single quotes, I am emphasizing that the noisetool represents only an idea or concept that resides in the mind... in a particular sentence or thought of the mind. Single quotes emphasizes that the idea or concept underlying a noisetool is only a 'thing' of the mind. Thus, the sign 'tree' (in single quotes), at any one moment, signals (or elicits) unique 'things' with their definitions (in the mind).

On the other hand, as noticed, the noisetool "tree" can be used to indicate something that is not of the mind's ideas or concepts. That TREE at which we are looking, does, in fact, have its own unique EXISTENCE, independent of any mind's thoughts, definitions, or descriptions. If it were possible for the billions of minds of EARTH to behold that TREE, all at the same spacemoment, for the BEING that IT is, there would be, at least, that many mental 'trees' representing the TREE. [And, of course, a remarkable global shift in consciousness would have also taken place, making this manual curiously unnecessary!]

Using single quotes and capital letters, herein, is a literary convention for helping readers to practice being all-HERE.

Any one individual will have only her or his own 'tree' for a TREE, and yet, in pure-EXISTENCE, that TREE will have a profusion of its own RELATIONSHIPS or CONNECTIONS within the FOREST or, by extension, within the ECOLOGIES about IT. Whatever unique appreciations, attributes, descriptions, purposes, or utilities a human may have for her or his own 'tree', all those RELATIONSHIPS would, nevertheless, still stand on their own within the

GREATER COMMUNITY of LIFE on EARTH. In its own way, the TREE exists as a part of a GREATER SYSTEM that is LIFE on EARTH. The TREE helps perpetuate that LIFE. Those RELATIONSHIPS are not contained by words, language or thought. Rather, they are woven into the unknowable and mysterious FABRIC of LIFE. In that we are ultimately dependent on this FABRIC for our own survival, it is essential that we keep IT in awe, that we revere ITS LIFE, that we know that IT is ever HERE within a COMMUNITY of other BEINGS, all WHO exist beyond our symbols, concepts, and thoughts, beyond our paradigms and enterprises.

As you see, I put a word all in capital letters when I wish to indicate the awesome EXISTENCE of the THING or BEING for which it stands. Such THINGS and BEINGS exist HERE, beyond the ideas or concepts pretending to define THEM. All THINGS and BEINGS have their own intrinsic, substantial INTEGRITY independent of the confines of human thought and representation.

Thus, as a receiver of the mind's projections, a THING or BEING remains, nevertheless, always within ITS own INTEGRITY. In deploying a mental 'thing' in order to define a THING/BEING, while trying to capture or enclose IT within our indexed thoughts, we lose sight of that ineffable INTEGRITY. We are unable to recognize the mental 'thing' as just a product of our own mind-induced systems of language, systems that do not have any 'thing' to do with that original INTEGRITY. When we try to define a mental 'event' or 'thing', we are simply defining according to the impressions, experiences, and purposes of our own heads. It's important to know the above distinctions.

▶**The 'tree' in my mind is never equivalent to the TREE out HERE.**

Too many human beings tend to take the 'things' of mind for granted, as though those 'things' were identical to the STUFF of EXISTENCE. Yet, such mental 'things' are only personal creations, creations generated from personal impressions (from sensations, images, visualizations, experiences, representations, symbolizations, deliberations, and ruminations), all of which are made in personal minds, in personal biocomputers, there to be indexed by our personal collections of words, and then, thereby, used to create the personal theaters of living that deal, almost exclusively, with human purposes and utilities.

At this point, I would like to suggest that the reader tack the phrase "beyond thought" on to any words placed in capital letters in this manual. By so doing, s/he should get used to this convention and should find that it helps facilitate her/his way to being all-HERE, to being entirely HERE-beyond-thought.

All THINGS and BEINGS exist, in their purity, beyond thought. THEY all have their own

SUBSTANTIAL-CONDITIONS regardless of 'what' we think of THEM. THEY are never identical to the mind's conceptions, to the indexed images, to the noisetooled, beworded thoughts of mind.

To summarize: The stylistic effect of using single quotes or capital letters with certain words is intended to remind the reader that language tends to limit the reader to the reader's own linguistic limits and habits (to her/his own conceptual parameters and paradigms). The ultimate EXISTENCE of all THINGS and BEINGS exists beyond mind, beyond the mechanics of language and thought. It is essential that we so-called "humans" come to appreciate that these substantial CONDITIONS are always impossible to capture in or convey by the 'things' of mind.

▶We must ever keep in mind that we never know the THINGS and BEINGS of pure-EXISTENCE, for we can only ever know 'things' of mind.

Now that the previous conventions are explained, the following sentence should be more easily appreciated for its bearing:

In many respects, the noisetool 'tree' is dangerous to the well-being of the FOREST, causing many to not see the FOREST for their own 'trees'.

...

A Discussion of Reification (Thingification)

Throughout the course of our struggle to subsist and, especially, since the introduction of language to our ways, we BEINGS have been caused to <u>project</u> the contents of our minds on to the WORLD, UNIVERSE, and SPACE about us. Of course, we do use our senses to negotiate EXISTENCE with sufficient alacrity to sponsor continued subsistence. Yet, 'what' we remember of our sensing is often so filtered and altered by the cognitive-linguistic processes of mind, to an embarrassing degree, we are caused to think merely per the abstract particulars of mental products that we end up projecting upon the STUFF of EXISTENCE. Those products that we take to have <u>high correlation</u> with the STUFF are 'things' that are so **reified**, we come to think and function as though they were "real" 'things'. Add enough of these *real* 'things' together and the mind devolves into a matrix that imprisons the psyche of one's BEING.

The following defines the term 'reify' or 'thingify':

> The term 'reify' (or its English twin 'thingify') is not used in everyday speech. This is unfortunate; for it is one of the most valuable words in use and should be a part of the vernaculars of all peoples. It is a Latin-based word. "Re-" comes from the Latin 'res' which in English signifies 'thing'. The "ify" is derived from 'facio' which translates as "to make".

Thus, the literal meaning of 'reify' translates as "to make into a thing".

To reify is defined as the process of considering an abstraction (a perception, an image, a thought, an indexed 'thing') of the mind to be identical to a concrete THING of pure-EXISTENCE. When an EVENT, THING, or BEING is perceived, IT is converted into an abstraction of the mind. When this abstraction is named and fit into human linguistic systems of thought, it is said to be "reified" or "thingified" when the mental 'thing' is, henceforth, misvalued as being "real" or, more precisely, as being *thought* to exist in EXISTENCE as it is conceived to be in mind. In other words, reification is the dysfunctional process of projecting the 'things' of mind on to THINGS and BEINGS, or on to SPACE or EXISTENCE.

Reification has three ways to raise its ugly head. First of all, some 'thing' of mind is projected upon an (apparently) inanimate THING. An example of this is seen when someone refers to some THING as a 'long bone' (which is good for keeping others away from your food). The second way, is encountered when some 'thing' is projected upon a BEING. An example of this is seen when someone refers to a BEING as an 'enemy' (who is likely to hit someone with a long bone in order to take food). The third and most peculiar way is demonstrated when a 'thing' of mind is projected upon the empty SPACE of EXISTENCE. In this third practice, there is no THING or BEING visible to receive the projection. There is no THING there that could even be a referent for the named 'thing'. A long practiced example of this kind of projecting is observed when someone says that it was not an enemy that took the food; but, it is was an angry 'god' who took it (for not having had its fill of the body and blood of human sacrifices for lunch). As time has pasted, this third kind of reified projection is still quite prevalent on our planet. Just look how kindergarten children can be seen arguing about the existence of Santa Clause or the Tooth Fairy, even to the point of coming to blows.

Many humans are still imagining that the conceptual 'things' conjured in mind can exist outside of mind. Just look at all the people who do not know that the term 'god' cannot exist without a mind to give it shape, all the people that find it so difficult to appreciate that mind-made 'things' do not exist outside of mind.

▶ **Will the one-and-only true 'god', please, step out of the mind!**

The list of 'things' that are projected upon empty SPACE or that don't have referents outside of mind is very long. Such 'things' pop up all over the planet. Our dictionaries house many an example of minor and major players who act upon the stages in the minds of our typical word-believing humans. I'll list some:

Spook, ghost, phantom, fairy, spirit, specter, god, devil, demon, bogie, angel, ogre, goblin, gnome, bugaboo, troll, and monster.

Often enough, terms like 'enemy' or 'terrorist' act in this third capacity. It is not uncommon for humans to imagine an enemy or terrorist that does not even have a referent anywhere. One can turn over many a stone and look behind many a telephone pole and not find any THING upon which to project the word 'enemy' or 'terrorist'. Of course, some so-called "leaders" just love having such 'enemies' and 'terrorists' about. It is easier to get people to do what one wants when people are fearful of some boogieman or, in this case, of some boogie-enemy.

If we look about our planet, we can find people who are really angry and willing to fight for their outrage. Some people just don't like having bombs dropped on their villages, for instance. But, it takes a manipulator to call them "enemy" or "terrorist". And, it seems, that our world still has plenty of manipulators who would continue to use our young people as fodder for their killing fields, so they can get what they want. Oh, well, such are the Machiavellian ways of those who intentionally use reifications to fool we-the-people of this WORLD.

All-in-all, when reified or seen as "real", a mental 'thing' is not readily questionable. Its validity as a "complete or perfect" depiction is not doubted; such doubt, often enough, does not even come to mind. So we see how reified 'things' are not seen as mere representations of human thought or of some human system of thinking.

Obviously, when a thought is thingified (reified), its contents become narrowly defined and rigidly used. Narrow definitions tend to exclude other potentially important (if not vital) relationships that THINGS and BEINGS might have amongst THEMSELVES. As mentioned in the following Thesis, an orchid can go extinct because of how some human reified purposes can incidentally disrupt the plant's ecological niche.

When human reified evaluations are used to consider the biological and ecological systems of a planet, they are deadly. BEINGS with their interrelations are not beheld or considered for WHAT they are beyond and outside of human conceptualizations, purposes, and utilities. Thus, the large fish of the oceans are being decimated by predators in enormous boats and their dependent ecological niches are being disrupted. Such is the cause of many an extinction.

...

An Introduction to the Reification-Extinction Thesis

"Welcome to the Gardens of Earth, but remember, the day that you bite into the fruit of the tree of the knowledge of fixed ideas, of mental absolutes—like, for instance, the notion of 'good' versus 'evil'—will be the day that you'll be kicked out of the garden! So there! You've been warned!"

—Some guy with a fiery sword

Please, imagine it's the mid 1960's and I am floating about the inner space of the University of Wisconsin Madison campus. I am feeling rather foreign to the world beyond these hallowed halls, rather like an alien scientist looking at a peculiar oddity in a newly discovered solar system. Because of my involvement in the burgeoning ecology movement, I am preoccupied with a major concern: how is it that these beings called "human" are causing an ongoing, widespread mass-extinction of life-forms on this third planet of this solar system? How is it that these humans are destroying the very ecological systems that sustain them?

Part of my work involves writing about that question and one of my fliers—a short essay—seems to be of particular interest to a black-suited gentleman who asks me to talk to a group he represents. I show up on the designated day to speak. And, what a strange meeting it is. I am to speak to a darkened room below me, where each member of this group is sitting at his own little table, the surface of which is lit by a little lamp with a flexible neck. The rest of the room is dark and I cannot make out anyone's features. Upon sizing up the situation, I do what I have come to do. I begin to speak:

> "You people do not know what you are doing! The Hudson River is dead. [A very large number, no longer remembered] of gallons of industrial effluent are being dumped into the river per day. Thank you very much."

In that I had been set up to speak under false pretenses, this short delivery seems to suffice. I sit back down next to Mr. Black Suit and ask, "How did I do?" He says, "Very well." I do not look at him again.

The above mentioned flier that drew so much attention was called "Revolutionary Talk". Within it lay the rudiments of the Reification-Extinction Thesis. It was not until the mid 80's that I finally wrote the thesis down. Publishing it did not seem to matter. I was too busy going down the path of a self-induced spiritual journey—one that preoccupied the surplus effort of my psyche.

In the late summer of 1983, while visiting the United States-Canadian boundary waters, the conspicuously pristine aspect of the area made itself spiritually and physically visible to my consciousness. I had a major epiphany. In one memorable event, while looking deeply into a mound of unnamed mosses, an epiphany (or "satori", as I came to call it) transformed my person into a BEING that would henceforth be conscious of being an unnamable BEING.

Yet, now, I had to understand the import of that event. I had to get my head around it. And, so, ever since that momentous day, my BEING has been on a new journey, one of trying to write about being a BEING and, subsequently, about how I may help other BEINGS to actualize themselves as such. The words that remain of my journey will hopefully improve the journeys of those who are also seeking to live genuinely, so to be their most authentic and fullest BEING.

The Reification-Extinction Thesis

Concerning the Recent Mass Extinction

on Planet Earth

By Professor BEING

Synopsis:

The effects of reification within the cognitive systems of the Homo sapiens sapiens are cumulatively causing a mass extinction (called the Anthropocene Extinction) of many forms of LIFE on the planet Earth.

The Thesis:

The purpose of this report is to present a thesis that would present the most basic cause of the current Anthropocene Extinction. It suggests that a collapse of the planet's otherwise sustainable ecological interactions is being induced by a deleterious process that is inherent to the linguistic-cognitive practices of the human being. Herein, this process is being called "reification":

The cumulative effects of a species-wide process of reification within the general cognitions (thinking processes) of the Homo sapiens sapiens—by an ever growing, expanding, and consumptive population—is constituting an overspecialization that is causing a mass extinction within the speciation of the ecologies of Earth.

[Terms used in this thesis are examined, presently.]

Recently, the population growth of the self-dubbed "human being"—the "Homo sapiens sapiens" in academic parlance—has markedly accelerated. In roughly two centuries, its population has increased seven fold, from around 1 billion in 1800 to around 7 billion today. By 2050 it is likely to exceed 9 billion (9 fold in 250 years). As this life-form's demand for exclusive living-space expands, as its use of living and non-living resources encroaches upon the ecologies of other life-forms, normal or typical ecological checks and balances have given way to processes that are causing mass extinction. Without self-imposed population and consumption controls, it appears as though the impact of such expansion—into the ecological living-spaces of most other forms of LIFE—will continue to cause one of the most wide-spread mass extinctions to ever have occurred on the planet.

<>< Note ><>

As purportedly embodying greater sagacity, the Homo sapiens sapiens is not, in fact, proving to be very "sapient" as to its dependence upon the ecologies of Earth.

<><><>

Some terms used in this thesis need definition:

Reification: Reflecting what is stated above, the processes of reification involve the tendency of taking thoughts—which are, in fact, never more than abstract 'things', symbolic, representational, cognitive structures of mind—as though they were equivalent to the "real", "concrete" THINGS of pure-EXISTENCE.

For example, the concept 'white man' may be thought to exist outside of mind; even though this is totally an absurd proposition. 'White man' (or, say, 'black man' or 'red man') can exist only as a concept, only in minds. And, yet, the typical *human being* (in itself, another reification) acts as though such abstract 'things' exist as concrete THINGS, and, this, nearly all the time. Thus, BEINGS are divided unnecessarily into different camps that seem ever too ready for prejudicial discrimination and, of course, eventual violence.

As pointed out, herein, all kinds of violence are the result of the employment of reifications. Thus, whole regions of FORESTS are reified as collections of 'trees' that are deemed to be composed of 'wood', which is to be exchanged for 'money', 'profit', and 'power'. The violence performed against such regions is astounding, yet, often goes nearly unnoticed.

With regard to the potential thinker, the reification of thoughts precludes an awareness of the non-symbolic, non-verbal, unthought THINGS and BEINGS falling outside of the indexings of language. With respect to the BEING called "human being", the concept of 'human being' (as with 'white man', 'red man', 'black man', etc.) is a major reification that prevents the BEING-called-human from recognizing that IT is a

BEING among BEINGS and that such BEINGS all reside within a greater, holistic SYSTEM that, in-ITSELF, ever remains unconceptualized and undivided by any reified 'things' of thought or mind. Thus, reifications prevent BEINGS from awakening to or being conscious of their own widespread, integral BEINGNESS. Of course, such unconsciousness leads to severe exploitations which adversely impact biological systems, as noted when FORESTS are reified into 'forests of trees' to be, henceforth, seen as just so much 'wood', etc..

Overspecialization: Per those processes of reification functioning within the use of language, it appears that the human being has entered into an overspecialization. An overspecialization occurs when a species takes on an adaptive specialization that has an adverse effect upon the potential for its survival within the ecological niche or living mechanisms of the species. That is to say, the survival of the species is put into jeopardy. Normally, an overspecialization is considered to be fixed and irreversible; because, it is locked in place by genetic and environmental relationships that have evolved within the interdependencies of a life-form's environs, its ecological niche. These genetic-environmental relationships can be said to be "hardwired" and, therefore, beyond the adaptability of the life-form to undo.

For example, let's consider a flower, an orchid that reproduces with the help of a butterfly. The butterfly performs "sex" for the flower by carrying pollen from flower to flower. In that the flower cannot have sex without the butterfly, it is said to be overspecialized with respect to its mechanisms of procreation. If, for some reason, the butterfly is unable to be present for the flower, the flower will go extinct. Or, conversely, if that butterfly gets its food solely from that flower and that flower is no longer available, then, in like manner, the butterfly will go extinct. However, if the butterfly is not overspecialized with respect to getting its food only from the flower, thus, having alternative sources, it is said that the butterfly is not overspecialized with respect to its food supply. The flower would be only one of its sources for sustenance. Another example of overspecialization is the koala bear's dependence on the (undisturbed) eucalyptus tree for food and shelter. If the eucalyptus becomes too scarce or unavailable, its nutritional overspecialization will cause its extinction. There are many overspecializations in LIFE on Earth. The elephant is definitely overspecialized with respect to its dependence on vast areas for grazing and, as with many other life-forms, its environs are being adversely limited by human encroachment.

Another type of overspecialization is also made possible by circumstances that are not necessarily directly "locked-in" by the genetic makeup of a species. A species that adversely affects its environs via mechanisms that are determined predominantly by fixed "habits" may be said to be "soft-wired" into manifesting an overspecialization. Although, such habits are potentially changeable or manageable, in that humans may be too slow to change fundamental habits, in that they may be unresponsive to pressures for change, a soft-wired overspecialization may cause such great damage to the environs of the human that the extinction of the Homo sapiens sapiens may follow with high probability.

To continue the use of computer metaphors, an animal may manage its 'software processes' or 'mental programmings' with respect to its observable—closed or open—ecological system. Yet, such a life-form needs to have the capacity or intelligence for such management.

...

Because of its abundant water and other elemental constituents and because of its favorable distance from a star, called "The Sun", the planet Earth is ideally suited for LIFE. That distance, averaging approximately 93 million miles, allows the Earth with the aid of its biological support systems to maintain a range of temperatures and climatic conditions that are conducive to a potentially luxuriant growth of LIVING-SYSTEMS.

It appears that the Homo sapiens sapiens is at a crucial stage in its evolution. In that the human being's cognitive mechanisms for survival utilize symbolic systems (called language) to interface with its resources for survival, much depends upon how the human being manages the software of its symbolic systems. Unfortunately, it is likely that in the early development of the use of symbolic systems, life-forms may tend to be unconsciously inflexible with regard to managing their cognitions. They may be unaware of how to manage language with respect to the optimal sustainability of interdependent systems, especially, those systems upon which they are dependent. In the case of the human being, the relatively recent development of the scientific method is demonstrating greater sophistication in the use of symbols within scientific and technological endeavors. However, it is not predictable whether the governing elements of the human population will have the sophistication to educate themselves and their charges as to the deleterious effects of the wide-spread processes of reification in time to head-off a critically expansive extinction on the planet.

For the most part, it seems that humans remain spiritually, psychologically, sociologically, economically, politically, and environmentally unprepared for managing symbols for their own long-term welfare. They seem to be rather myopic and rigid in their ways, ways that do not predominantly consider the biological systems of their planet. As "civilized" life-forms that depend heavily upon the symbols for managing their utilities, humans seem prone to reifying aspects of their thinking to the exclusion of thinking systemically about the ecological systems within which they live. In other words, they exploit their 'resources' without regard to how their resources constitute interdependent elements in the webs of LIFE around them. They use 'things' without regard to maintaining an appreciation for the LIVING-SYSTEMS that perpetuate the LIFE of the BIOSPHERE of their planet. They allow their symbolic systems to concentrate upon their immediate needs while perpetuating wide-spread ignorance as to the needs of their planet's biological systems.

The damage of this wide-spread ignorance is compounded by the wide-spread ignorance of how the processes of cognitive abstraction are obscured by the deleterious processes of reification. The long-evolved LIVING-SYSTEMS seem to be far from the consciousness of the typical every-day citizen involved in trying to survive within the economies of civil existence. Sadly, such ignorance frames outlooks which prove to be disruptive to a planet's ecologies. At this point in the evolution of Homo sapiens sapiens, it is difficult to determine whether a sufficient number of human beings will be able to see the errors of their reified 'ways' in time to stop a complete collapse of a vast majority of the biological systems of Earth's BIOSPHERE.

Under the auspices of using languages, humans have generated mental paradigms that interface in rudimentary ways with the resources of their planet. Many a life-form and biological system is affected by these paradigms. Wherever one looks one can see how the paradigms of human languages impact the Earth's environs.

All paradigms are limited in scope. One can leave out important details and, at the same time, include irrelevant or invalid ones. For instance, the paradigm involving 'trees-wood-lumber-money-profit' can cause a life-form that is otherwise completely integrated within its natural system to appear insular or isolated. One such life-form is called a "redwood tree". For the reified concept of 'redwood', this life-form is treated as not being integral to the LIFE of once vast and venerable LIVING-SYSTEMS containing multitudes of BEINGS. Such a paradigm defines this life-form in terms that are so incomplete that the exploitation is leading to the extermination of many life-forms.

Continuing a previous example, the elephant cannot be defined adequately without considering the vast stretches of territory necessary to its survival. Yet, even though territorial encroachment could easily enough cause its extinction, the elephant's extinction may come for another reason. It may come as the results of a word: 'ivory'. The illegal ivory trade is so lucrative, populations of elephants are slaughtered merely for the 'ivory' of their trunks.

Unfortunately, language too often lends itself to categorical and, thus, insular thinking, while life-forms are always parts of vastly integrated, interdependent, and inter-being LIVING-SYSTEMS. To approach and adequately analyze such SYSTEMS, one needs to employ some form of "systems-thinking". Without such thinking, sustainable management is not possible. The first step towards such management is taken as we recognize that BEINGS do not reside in or as symbolic structures. Moreover, THEY cannot be represented on a one-to-one basis by the verbal elements of cognition. The 'tree' is not the TREE! If this is thought possible, the thinker would be approaching the circumstances of LIFE and BEING in a very unscientific manner. To reify any hypothesis is to defeat the one method that civilization has found to undo the dysfunctional processes of reification that so typically undermine what little intelligence we humans are able to muster. The reification of 'ivory' as an economically precious material demonstrates very well just how stupid humans can be vis-à-vis the survival of long-evolved and irreplaceable species.

...

Many life-forms are labeled, some are not. Those life-forms that have been labeled or indexed by words are, to varying extents, directly affected by them. Those that are not labeled are indirectly affected by human indexing and related behaviors. A labeling word is defined with just so many elementary, categorical constituents—just so many ingredients. Within such definitions, the word-user cannot help but see the labeled 'things' (of mind) as being separate or insular, ready for use and exploitation.

The behaviors dealing with such mental 'things' will demonstrate just to what extent the word-user is unconscious of the ecological connections (nexi) belonging to a life-form's ecologies. Very often life-forms are treated as though they had no ecological relations at all.

Whether labeled or unlabeled, *known* or *unknown*, life-forms are affected by how humans reduce THINGS and BEINGS to the 'things' of mind. Humans readily "bulldoze away" (figuratively and materially)—often without the least concern for long-standing ecological systems—WHAT does not fit the objectives developed for those mind-made 'things' designated for consumption. At this very moment, many of the "unknowns" of the natural WORLD are being inadvertently liquidated as the short-term objectives of human paradigms are reflected in human actions. Unless humans go out of their own 'ways' to see the interconnections and vital interdependencies that exist out HERE in the LIVING-WORLD, they do not treat that WORLD as though IT were indeed "living". To the conscious BEING, the word 'living' here will suggest that the THINGS and BEINGS of this WORLD are constituents of integrated LIVING-SYSTEMS. However, it appears that the typical human word-user is not readily aware of the interconnections of LIFE. Moreover, not having a means to express what is to happen to these LIVING-SYSTEMS, non-human life-forms have no means to defend their SYSTEMS and, thus, must endure the misfortune of being reduced to the 'things' of the human mind without any recourse. Most humans seem oblivious to the interconnections in such SYSTEMS.

And, thus, the interconnections are inadvertently severed; they are broken and the LIVING-SYSTEMS die—without any human necessarily knowing of it. When humans insert a new road into a forest or jungle, they seem to be unaware that such a road must inevitably bring in its wake new activities that will break long-standing ecological relationships. Thus, the ever-occurring extinctions—caused by humans—continue to go horrifically onward... while humans go on joy-rides down newly laid and paved roads. Et cetera, und so weiter, and so on.

Long-evolved LIVING-SYSTEMS continue to fall victim to the categorical activities of unconscious word-users. When sentient beings act upon a BIOSPHERE from the vantages of narrowly-defined labels, according to the pursuits of specified interests, purposes, and utilities, they cannot help but to "unconsciously" mistreat that BIOSPHERE.

It is impossible to co-exist with other life-forms when they are forced to live and die according to the definitions of reified labels and projections. As suggested, the affixed labels cannot aid in the preservation of LIVING-SYSTEMS, unless word-users come to think as systems-thinkers—thinkers who are aware that the mind makes representational or hypothetical structures (mental 'maps') of mental data. Of course, such thinkers are aware that there is never perfect representation of the pure-EXISTENCE of any THING, BEING, or LIVING-SYSTEM. Although the potential for preserving the survival of LIVING-SYSTEMS is improved by continually upgrading mental 'maps', nevertheless, it is most important to hold these SYSTEMS ever in awe and reverence, so as to not irreversibly disrupt their living functions.

The labels of ordinary language are too easily affixed to the specimens of LIFE. They too easily act to divide the WHOLE into separate categories. The labels disrupt the functions of the WHOLE and, often enough, cause word-users to be unable to recognize that the WHOLE even exists. As the WHOLE is divided into 'parts' by the mind's labels, concepts, and imposed programs, as the 'parts' are *canned* into the classifications of reified symbols, the WHOLE is too often lost to view. Were the labelers to add the 'parts' into 'sums', they would find the 'sums' always less than the WHOLE that comprises the LIVING-SYSTEMS of this planet. Thus, the appropriate approach to all LIVING-SYSTEMS is to behold them with awe and reverence, thereby, to act in stewardship for THEM.

...

Unaccustomed to seeing thought as the management of abstractions, symbols, or "mental 'maps'", the typical human, desiring personal security, is persuaded to establish the representations of mind as though they were fixed and invariable 'realities'. Going down such invariable 'ways' leads only to behavioral inflexibilities. As long as the human being is unaware that the mind can contain no more than the incidental 'things' representing the virtual processes of mind and that these 'things' are, therefore, never equivalent to pure-EXISTENCE, it will find itself with no ways back or no ways out of its dead-end 'ways', those leading to extinction. Such 'ways' provide the means for reifying whole paradigms of human cognition. Most egregiously, within these 'ways', the interdependencies of LIFE remain unnoticed and unattended and, therefore, these 'civilized ways' must infringe upon the ecologies of Earth.

Up to the more recent development of language, the human being's actions were much less dominant and impactful with regard to the BIOSPHERE. With the establishment of language, the human started to store and disseminate information, called "knowledge", that would prove to have cumulative effects upon its environs. With this accumulation it was able to expand its functional niche to include vast areas, expanded sources of food, more proficient safeguards against predation and disease, and the elimination of other threats, like the effects of adverse weather and climate. All these changes affect the survival of other life-forms, often leading to their extinction.

What is it about language use that can cause such advantages and, yet, eventually and unfortunately, the disadvantage of run-away population growth, environmental degradation, and, finally, an overspecialization, that would be the precursor and cause of extinction?:

As suggested, thinking-systems (symbolic, cognitive systems) allow "mapping" of sensory and cognitive data, permitting the collection of information which, in turn, permits a life-form to establish mechanisms for more readily exploiting its environs. Of course, without adequate awareness, overview, and consequent ability to adapt, exploitation proves to be detrimental in the long-run. Whatever may cause a lack of awareness for how the use of a symbolic-system can impact environmental conditions, it is quite evident that a sentient life-form can fall victim to a specialization that subsequently causes extinctions. Such circumstances are exacerbated as the specialization moves towards being overspecialized and irreversible.

The thesis herein presented suggests that the reification of the elements of human cognition is causing such a "whatever". The reifications of the 'things' of mind, by an ever-growing population, is ever causing greater unawareness, lack of overview, dangerous inflexibility, and an over-all inability to adapt to and to sustain viable, long-term relations with the biological systems of the planet Earth.

Summary of Thesis:

Life-forms can experience phases of rapid growth. Normally, there are impediments to the biotic potential or growth of an organism built into the checks and balances of ecological systems. However, varying factors can cause environmental conditions to change such that rampant and accelerating population growth occurs. In the case of the human being, those conditions are being instigated and perpetuated— primarily—by the adoption of mechanisms of language that fix in place previous indexings of mental 'things' and, thus, information ("knowledge") is passed down—from one generation to the next—in relatively fixed or traditional 'ways'. Secondarily—by the unfortunate consequence of a dysfunctional use of language-based thinking called "reification", these 'ways' are constituting an overspecialization that is causing mass extinction.

As we humans confuse the utilitarian 'things' of mind with what is necessary for survival, the THINGS and BEINGS of EXISTENCE are being removed from view and consciousness. For instance, as we confuse 'things' like 'human being' with our own BEING or 'trees' and 'wood' (etc.) with the marvels of those

LIVING-BEINGS of FORESTS, we reify away the wondrously complex manifestations of LIFE. As the reifications of our linguistic cognitions continue to cause the use of rigid, shortsighted, and non-inclusive paradigms with their short-term utilizations and exploitations, we humans continue to squeeze other life-forms out of EXISTENCE.

With this in mind the following proviso is stated:

Unless the individuals comprising the species called "Homo sapiens sapiens" are able to dereify their processes of cognition sufficiently to open them to being utilized as symbolic processes for shaping paradigms or representational systems, the LIVING-SYSTEMS of a planet will continue to be assaulted and disrupted.

The elements of this thesis may be outlined as follows:

1. The invention and use of language have made it possible for the self-named "human being" to create specializations that have permitted conditions for greater, more proficient exploitation, of living and nonliving resources.

2. The habit of reifying thoughts (cognitions)—of replacing the THINGS and BEINGS of pure-EXISTENCE with the reified structures of thought—is cementing such specializations into a vast overspecialization such that the human is largely

unable to alter the mechanisms and effects of those overspecializations.

3. Exacerbated by uncontrolled and ever accelerating population growth and consequent patterns of resource use—this overspecialization is causing a mass extinction within the BIOSPHERE of the planet.

4. This observer opines that the above progression is not hardwired (or hardwared) into the genetic/physiological conditions of being human, rather, that the occurrence of the wide-spread extinctions is caused by a softwiring (a softwaring) engendered by the reifications inherent to the linguistic habits/practices of human thinking (by the dysfunctional employment of language-based, human softwares and utilitarian systems). The use of language is not the problem, the reification of the elements of language is.

5. Reification can be eliminated (as are diseases) within the broader population, as it has (nearly) been within the sciences and technologies of Earth. However, this will require both financial and intellectual resources to do so.

6. Proper management with regard to the long-term sustainability of the current biological systems and BIOSPHERE of Earth can be employed.

When the THINGS and BEINGS of EXISTENCE are treated as though they are equivalent to the categories of language and thought, it follows that THEY will be acted upon according to the reasoned and purposeful processes currently underlying the actions. Without adequate science, such processes are likely to be rigid, unadaptive, and unresponsive to redirection.

In order to improve awareness of the underlying causes of our rigid and dysfunctional relations with the Earth's ecological systems, especially, vis-à-vis the phenomenon of the current global mass extinction, this thesis offers the term "reification". The process of for increasing awareness is called "dereification". The book The PhoB: The Philosophy of BEING offers various 'ways' to dereifying our relations with the beworded 'things' of human thought.

In that systems of thought do not and cannot adequately reflect any LIVING-SYSTEM, the BEINGS who are *being human* need to educate themselves, so to protect the viability and integrity of such SYSTEMS, this as though they were safeguarding the lives of their own families.

<><><>

Thank you for reading and considering this thesis.